# YOUR CHINESE HOROSCOPE FOR 1992

# YOUR CHINESE HOROSCOPE FOR 1992

What the Year of the Monkey
holds in store for you

## NEIL SOMERVILLE

The Aquarian Press
*An Imprint of* HarperCollins*Publishers*

The Aquarian Press
An Imprint of GraftonBooks
A Division of HarperCollins*Publishers*
77–85 Fulham Palace Road,
Hammersmith, London W6 8JB

Published by The Aquarian Press 1991

3 5 7 9 10 8 6 4 2

© Neil Somerville 1991

Neil Somerville asserts the moral right to
be identified as the author of this work.

A CIP record for this book is available from the British Library

ISBN 1-85538-062-5

Typeset by
Burns & Smith Ltd, Derby

Printed in Great Britain by
HarperCollinsManufacturing, Glasgow

# Contents

To Ros, Richard and Emily

# Introduction

The origins of Chinese horoscopes have been lost in the mists of time. It is known that oriental astrologers practised their art many thousands of years ago and, even today, Chinese astrology continues to fascinate and intrigue.

In Chinese astrology there are twelve signs named after twelve different animals. No one quite knows how the signs acquired their names, but there is one legend that offers an explanation.

According to this legend, one Chinese New Year, the Buddha invited all the animals in his kingdom to come before him. Unfortunately—for reasons best known to the animals—only twelve turned up. The first to arrive was the Rat, followed by the Ox, Tiger, Rabbit, Dragon, Snake, Horse, Goat, Monkey, Rooster, Dog and finally the Pig.

In gratitude, the Buddha decided to name a year after each of the animals and those born during that year would inherit some of the personality of that animal. Therefore those born in the year of the Ox would be hard working, resolute, and stubborn—just like the Ox; those born in the year of the Dog would be loyal and faithful—just like the Dog.

While not everyone can possibly share all the characteristics of a sign, it is incredible what similarities do occur, and this is partly where the fascination of Chinese horoscopes lies.

In addition to the twelve signs of the Chinese zodiac there are also five elements and these have a strengthening or moderating influence upon the sign. Details about the effects of the elements are described in each of the chapters on the twelve signs.

To find out which sign you were born under, refer to the tables on pages 9–11. As the Chinese year is based on the lunar year and does not start until late January or early February, it is particularly important for anyone born in those two months to check carefully the dates of the Chinese year in which they were born.

Also included, in the appendix, are two charts showing the compatibility between the signs for both personal and business relationships, and details about the signs ruling the different hours of the day. From this it is possible to locate your ascendant and, as in Western astrology, this has a significant influence on your personality.

In writing this book, I have taken the unusual step of combining the intriguing nature of Chinese horoscopes with the Western desire to know what the future holds and have based my interpretations upon various factors relating to each of the signs. This is the fifth year in which *Your Chinese Horoscope* has been published and I am pleased that so many have found the sections on the forthcoming year of benefit and that the advice has been constructive and helpful. Remember, though, that at all times you are the master of your own destiny and I sincerely hope that your Chinese horoscope for 1992 will prove interesting and helpful for the year ahead.

# The Chinese Years

| Rat | 31 January | 1900 | to | 18 February | 1901 |
|---|---|---|---|---|---|
| Ox | 19 February | 1901 | to | 7 February | 1902 |
| Tiger | 8 February | 1902 | to | 28 January | 1903 |
| Rabbit | 29 January | 1903 | to | 15 February | 1904 |
| Dragon | 16 February | 1904 | to | 3 February | 1905 |
| Snake | 4 February | 1905 | to | 24 January | 1906 |
| Horse | 25 January | 1906 | to | 12 February | 1907 |
| Goat | 13 February | 1907 | to | 1 February | 1908 |
| Monkey | 2 February | 1908 | to | 21 January | 1909 |
| Rooster | 22 January | 1909 | to | 9 February | 1910 |
| Dog | 10 February | 1910 | to | 29 January | 1911 |
| Pig | 30 January | 1911 | to | 17 February | 1912 |
| Rat | 18 February | 1912 | to | 5 February | 1913 |
| Ox | 6 February | 1913 | to | 25 January | 1914 |
| Tiger | 26 January | 1914 | to | 13 February | 1915 |
| Rabbit | 14 February | 1915 | to | 2 February | 1916 |
| Dragon | 3 February | 1916 | to | 22 January | 1917 |
| Snake | 23 January | 1917 | to | 10 February | 1918 |
| Horse | 11 February | 1918 | to | 31 January | 1919 |
| Goat | 1 February | 1919 | to | 19 February | 1920 |
| Monkey | 20 February | 1920 | to | 7 February | 1921 |
| Rooster | 8 February | 1921 | to | 27 January | 1922 |
| Dog | 28 January | 1922 | to | 15 February | 1923 |
| Pig | 16 February | 1923 | to | 4 February | 1924 |
| Rat | 5 February | 1924 | to | 24 January | 1925 |
| Ox | 25 January | 1925 | to | 12 February | 1926 |
| Tiger | 13 February | 1926 | to | 1 February | 1927 |
| Rabbit | 2 February | 1927 | to | 22 January | 1928 |
| Dragon | 23 January | 1928 | to | 9 February | 1929 |

| | | | | | |
|---|---|---|---|---|---|
| Snake | 10 February | 1929 | to | 29 January | 1930 |
| Horse | 30 January | 1930 | to | 16 February | 1931 |
| Goat | 17 February | 1931 | to | 5 February | 1932 |
| Monkey | 6 February | 1932 | to | 25 January | 1933 |
| Rooster | 26 January | 1933 | to | 13 February | 1934 |
| Dog | 14 February | 1934 | to | 3 February | 1935 |
| Pig | 4 February | 1935 | to | 23 January | 1936 |
| Rat | 24 January | 1936 | to | 10 February | 1937 |
| Ox | 11 February | 1937 | to | 30 January | 1938 |
| Tiger | 31 January | 1938 | to | 18 February | 1939 |
| Rabbit | 19 February | 1939 | to | 7 February | 1940 |
| Dragon | 8 February | 1940 | to | 26 January | 1941 |
| Snake | 27 January | 1941 | to | 14 February | 1942 |
| Horse | 15 February | 1942 | to | 4 February | 1943 |
| Goat | 5 February | 1943 · | to | 24 January | 1944 |
| Monkey | 25 January | 1944 | to | 12 February | 1945 |
| Rooster | 13 February | 1945 | to | 1 February | 1946 |
| Dog | 2 February | 1946 | to | 21 January | 1947 |
| Pig | 22 January | 1947 | to | 9 February | 1948 |
| Rat | 10 February | 1948 | to | 28 January | 1949 |
| Ox | 29 January | 1949 | to | 16 February | 1950 |
| Tiger | 17 February | 1950 | to | 5 February | 1951 |
| Rabbit | 6 February | 1951 | to | 26 January | 1952 |
| Dragon | 27 January | 1952 | to | 13 February | 1953 |
| Snake | 14 February | 1953 | to | 2 February | 1954 |
| Horse | 3 February | 1954 | to | 23 January | 1955 |
| Goat | 24 January | 1955 | to | 11 February | 1956 |
| Monkey | 12 February | 1956 | to | 30 January | 1957 |
| Rooster | 31 January | 1957 | to | 17 February | 1958 |
| Dog | 18 February | 1958 | to | 7 February | 1959 |
| Pig | 8 February | 1959 | to | 27 January | 1960 |
| Rat | 28 January | 1960 | to | 14 February | 1961 |
| Ox | 15 February | 1961 | to | 4 February | 1962 |
| Tiger | 5 February | 1962 | to | 24 January | 1963 |
| Rabbit | 25 January | 1963 | to | 12 February | 1964 |
| Dragon | 13 February | 1964 | to | 1 February | 1965 |
| Snake | 2 February | 1965 | to | 20 January | 1966 |

| | | | | | |
|---|---|---|---|---|---|
| Horse | 21 January | 1966 | to | 8 February | 1967 |
| Goat | 9 February | 1967 | to | 29 January | 1968 |
| Monkey | 30 January | 1968 | to | 16 February | 1969 |
| Rooster | 17 February | 1969 | to | 5 February | 1970 |
| Dog | 6 February | 1970 | to | 26 January | 1971 |
| Pig | 27 January | 1971 | to | 14 February | 1972 |
| Rat | 15 February | 1972 | to | 2 February | 1973 |
| Ox | 3 February | 1973 | to | 22 January | 1974 |
| Tiger | 23 January | 1974 | to | 10 February | 1975 |
| Rabbit | 11 February | 1975 | to | 30 January | 1976 |
| Dragon | 31 January | 1976 | to | 17 February | 1977 |
| Snake | 18 February | 1977 | to | 6 February | 1978 |
| Horse | 7 February | 1978 | to | 27 January | 1979 |
| Goat | 28 January | 1979 | to | 15 February | 1980 |
| Monkey | 16 February | 1980 | to | 4 February | 1981 |
| Rooster | 5 February | 1981 | to | 24 January | 1982 |
| Dog | 25 January | 1982 | to | 12 February | 1983 |
| Pig | 13 February | 1983 | to | 1 February | 1984 |
| Rat | 2 February | 1984 | to | 19 February | 1985 |
| Ox | 20 February | 1985 | to | 8 February | 1986 |
| Tiger | 9 February | 1986 | to | 28 January | 1987 |
| Rabbit | 29 January | 1987 | to | 16 February | 1988 |
| Dragon | 17 February | 1988 | to | 5 February | 1989 |
| Snake | 6 February | 1989 | to | 26 January | 1990 |
| Horse | 27 January | 1990 | to | 14 February | 1991 |
| Goat | 15 February | 1991 | to | 3 February | 1992 |
| Monkey | 4 February | 1992 | to | 22 January | 1993 |

*Note*: The names of the signs in the Chinese zodiac occasionally differ in the various books on Chinese astrology, although the characteristics of that sign remain the same. In some books the Ox is referred to as the Buffalo or Bull, the Rabbit as the Hare or Cat, the Goat as the Sheep and the Pig as the Boar.

For the sake of convenience, the male gender is used throughout this book. Unless otherwise stated the characteristics of the signs apply to both sexes.

*Enlarge your heart to accommodate all things; empty your heart to receive the world's good; equalize your heart to observe the world's affairs; calm your heart to adjust to the world's changes.*

Chinese Proverb.

# Welcome to the Year of the Monkey

Whether viewed in its natural habitat, in a zoo, or on film, the Monkey is an undoubted star. Agile, distinctive and often so amusing to watch, the Monkey is a great entertainer and one that seems to command our attention. And so it is with the year of the Monkey—a year that will be dramatic and will offer many new and exciting opportunities.

The year of the Monkey starts on 4 February 1992. It has often been said that anything can happen in a Monkey year, and indeed some of the events that will occur in 1992 will be sudden and possibly turbulent.

Previous Monkey years this century (1908, 1920, 1932, 1944, 1956, 1968, and 1980) have been marked by the rise of nationalist movements, and it is likely that 1992 will be no exception. Many nationalist groups will be pressing their claims for independence, sovereignty and equal rights; it is likely that their actions could result in turmoil in several countries throughout the world, particularly those in Eastern Europe.

Monkey years have also been marked by acts of terrorism and violence, and while naturally it is hoped that this will not be the case in 1992, the threat cannot be ruled out. Monkey years have witnessed events such as the Hungarian uprising, the Suez crisis, the start of the Iran-Iraq war, and the clashes in Londonderry in October 1968 which caused a serious escalation of the troubles in Northern Ireland. The revolt by the Young Turks also occurred in a Monkey year, as did the 1968 student riots in Paris.

The year of the Monkey has also witnessed several

assassinations—Senator Robert Kennedy, Martin Luther King, John Lennon, Archbishop Romero and President Doumer of France were all assassinated in Monkey years.

Although this may make sombre reading, the governments of the world will be more united in their actions in 1992, and bodies such as the United Nations will be active in trying to solve disputes and bring a sense of reason to some of the trouble spots in the world. Several very important and far-reaching treaties will be signed during the year, so although 1992 could be turbulent at times, out of this turbulence will arise a greater understanding between the nations of the world. Indeed, as the Chinese philosopher Lao-tzu observed, 'What may appear to be a calamity often gives rise to fortune.'

The Monkey year 1992 will see a milestone reached in the history of Europe with the creation of a single European market. This will almost certainly prove of significant advantage to most European nations, although with the creation of this vast market, 1992 could be marked by a series of bureaucratic problems, brought on by the difficulties certain companies and organizations will have in adjusting to new regulations. The financial markets throughout the world are likely to behave fairly erratically in 1992, and will certainly not be helped by pressures brought to bear on the price of metals, oil, and raw materials.

There have been many industrial disputes in Monkey years, and the problems of industrial relations are going to loom large on the agenda of many governments throughout the world. However, although Monkey years can be challenging ones, there are nevertheless some positive and encouraging aspects to look forward to in 1992.

The year will see some major advances in science and technology. New and important pieces of technology will be developed, and scientists will enjoy considerable success in harnessing sources of alternative energy. Interest and concern about the environment and ecological matters will continue unabated, and some governments and international organizations will take major steps to reduce the manufacture and use of harmful gases and other pollutants.

Monkey years have in the past seen the start or completion of many major building projects, and 1992 will be no exception. The world's longest road tunnel, running over 16km under the St Gotthard Range in Switzerland, was opened in a Monkey year. Other Monkey years have seen the completion of the Zuider Zee drainage project, the Aswan Dam, and the opening of Sydney Harbour bridge. Britain's first atomic power station at Calder Hall was opened in a Monkey year, and it was also in that same year, 1956, that the Queen laid the foundation stone for Coventry cathedral.

On the international political scene, 1992 is a presidential election year in America, and after the primaries—which will offer several surprises—the election is likely to be one of the most keenly contested in recent years. However, should he seek re-election, George Bush (a Rat) is likely to emerge the eventual victor—Rats do tend to do well in Monkey years.

Although, as has been indicated, events throughout the world could prove a testing time for governments, for most individuals 1992 will offer many personal opportunities. It is a year to look at your objectives positively, a year to have confidence in yourself and make the best of your abilities and yourself. Monkey years favour creativity and enterprise, and for those who are prepared to act on their initiative the rewards can be very great indeed. Throughout 1992 there will certainly be plenty of opportunities for those who wish to pursue them.

This will be a year many will enjoy—the Monkey does, after all, have a delicious sense of humour, and he will ensure that we will be kept amused and entertained by some excellent new films, new trends in music, and some flamboyant and distinctive fashions.

It was in 1908, the year of the Monkey, when Robert Baden Powell founded the now internationally famous Boy Scout movement. The motto of the movement is 'Be prepared', and it is a very apt motto for us all to bear in mind for 1992. Be prepared, be bold and be positive—those who are, are likely to reap the many benefits that the year of the Monkey can offer.

In the pages that follow you will read about your own prospects for the year ahead. Naturally some signs will fare better than others, but even if your horoscope may not be as favourable as you would like, I have included at the end of each chapter an 'Action Plan for 1992', and in this plan I have indicated how I believe each of the signs can achieve the best results for the forthcoming year.

The year of the Monkey is sure to be an exciting and historic one, and I sincerely hope that it will be a successful and happy year for you.

# The Rat

| | | | |
|---|---|---|---|
| 31 January 1900 | to | 18 February 1901 | *Metal Rat* |
| 18 February 1912 | to | 5 February 1913 | *Water Rat* |
| 5 February 1924 | to | 24 January 1925 | *Wood Rat* |
| 24 January 1936 | to | 10 February 1937 | *Fire Rat* |
| 10 February 1948 | to | 28 January 1949 | *Earth Rat* |
| 28 January 1960 | to | 14 February 1961 | *Metal Rat* |
| 15 February 1972 | to | 2 February 1973 | *Water Rat* |
| 2 February 1984 | to | 19 February 1985 | *Wood Rat* |

## The Personality of the Rat

Life is too short to be little.
                    – *Benjamin Disraeli.*

The Rat is born under the sign of charm. He is intelligent, popular, and loves attending parties and large social gatherings. He is able to establish friendships with remarkable ease and people generally feel relaxed in his company. He is a very social creature and is genuinely interested in the welfare and activities of others. He has a good understanding of human nature and his advice and opinions are often sought.

The Rat is a hard and diligent worker. He is also very imaginative and is never short of ideas. However, he does sometimes lack the confidence to promote his ideas as much as he should and this can often prevent him from securing the recognition and credit he so often deserves.

The Rat is very observant and there are many who have made excellent writers and journalists. He also excels at personnel and PR work and any job which brings him into contact with people and the media. His skills are particularly appreciated in times of crisis, for the Rat has an incredibly strong sense of self-preservation. When it comes to finding a way out of an awkward situation, the Rat is certain to be the one who comes up with a solution.

The Rat loves to be where there is a lot of action, but should he ever find himself in a very bureaucratic or restrictive environment he can become a stickler for discipline and routine.

He is also something of an opportunist and is constantly on the look-out for ways in which he can improve his wealth and lifestyle. He rarely lets an opportunity go by and can become involved in so many plans and schemes that he sometimes squanders his energies and achieves very little as a result. He is also rather gullible and can be taken in by those less scrupulous than himself.

Another characteristic of the Rat is his attitude to money. He is very thrifty and to some he may appear a little mean. The reason for this is purely that he likes to keep his money within his family. He can be most generous to his partner, his children, and close friends and relatives. He can also be generous to himself, for he often finds it impossible to deprive himself of any luxury or object which he fancies. The Rat is also very acquisitive and can be a notorious hoarder. He hates waste and is rarely prepared to throw anything away. He can also be rather greedy and will rarely refuse an invitation for a free meal or a complimentary ticket to some lavish function.

The Rat is a good conversationalist, although he can occasionally be a little indiscreet. He can be highly critical of others—for an honest and unbiased opinion the Rat is a superb critic—and will use confidential information to his own advantage. However, as the Rat has such a bright and irresistible nature, most are prepared to forgive him for his slight indiscretions.

Throughout his long and eventful life, the Rat will make many friends and will find that he is especially well-suited to those born under his own sign and those of the Ox, Dragon, and Monkey. The Rat can also get on well with those born under the signs of the Tiger, Snake, Rooster, Dog, and Pig, but the rather sensitive Rabbit and Goat will find the Rat a little too critical and blunt for their liking. The Horse and Rat will also find it difficult to get on—the Rat craves for security and will find the Horse's changeable moods and rather independent nature a little unsettling.

The Rat is very family orientated and will do anything to please his nearest and dearest. He is exceptionally loyal to his parents and can himself be a very caring and loving parent. He will take an interest in all his children's activities and will see that they want for nothing. The Rat usually has a large family.

The female Rat has a kindly, outgoing nature and involves herself in a multitude of different activities. She is a superb hostess and will usually have a wide circle of very good friends. She is conscientious about the upkeep of her home and has superb taste in home furnishings. She is extremely supportive to the other members of her family and, due to her resourceful, friendly and persevering nature, can do well in practically any career she enters.

Although the Rat is essentially outgoing and something of an extrovert, he is also a very private individual. He tends to keep his feelings to himself and while he is not averse to learning what other people are doing, he resents anyone prying too closely into his own affairs. The Rat also does not like solitude and if he is alone for any length of time he can easily get depressed.

The Rat is undoubtedly very talented but more often

than not he fails to capitalize on his many abilities. He has a tendency to become involved in too many schemes and chase after too many opportunities all at one time. If he were to slow down and concentrate on one thing at a time he could become very successful. If not, success and wealth may elude him. But the Rat, with his tremendous ability to charm, will rarely, if ever, be without friends.

# The Five Different Types of Rat

In addition to the twelve signs of the Chinese zodiac, there are five elements, and these have a strengthening or moderating influence on the sign. The effects of the five elements on the Rat are described below, together with the years that the elements were exercising their influence. Therefore all Rats born in 1900 and 1960 are Metal Rats, those born in 1912 and 1972 are Water Rats, and so on.

**Metal Rat: 1900, 1960**
This Rat has excellent taste and certainly knows how to appreciate the finer things in life. His home is comfortable and nicely decorated and he is forever entertaining or mixing in fashionable circles. He has considerable financial acumen and invests his money well. On the surface the Metal Rat appears cheerful and confident, but deep down he can be troubled by worries that are quite often of his own making. He is exceptionally loyal to his family and friends.

**Water Rat: 1912, 1972**
The Water Rat is intelligent and very astute. He is a deep thinker and can express his thoughts clearly and persuasively. He is always eager to learn and is talented in many different areas. The Water Rat is usually very popular but his fear of loneliness can sometimes lead him into mixing with the wrong sort of company. He is a

particularly skilful writer, but he can get side-tracked very easily and should try to concentrate on just one thing at a time.

## Wood Rat: 1924, 1984
The Wood Rat has a friendly outgoing personality and is most popular with his colleagues and friends. He has a quick, agile brain and likes to turn his hand to anything he thinks may be useful. His one fear, however, is insecurity, but given his intelligence and capabilities this fear is usually unfounded. He has a good sense of humour, enjoys travel and, due to his highly imaginative nature, can be a gifted writer or artist.

## Fire Rat: 1936
The Fire Rat is rarely still and seems to have a never-ending supply of energy and enthusiasm. He loves being involved in the action—be it travel, following up new ideas, or campaigning for a cause in which he fervently believes. He is an original thinker and hates being bound by petty restrictions or the dictates of others. He can be forthright in his views, but can sometimes get carried away in the excitement of the moment and commit himself to various undertakings without checking what all the implications might be. He has a resilient nature and, with the right support, can often go far in life.

## Earth Rat: 1948
This Rat is astute and very level-headed. He rarely takes unnecessary chances and, while he is constantly trying to improve his financial status, he is prepared to proceed slowly and leave nothing to chance. The Earth Rat is probably not as adventurous as the other types of Rat and prefers to remain in areas he knows rather than rush headlong into something he knows little about. He is talented, conscientious, and caring towards his loved ones but at the same time can be self-conscious and worry too much about the image he is trying to project.

# Prospects for the Rat in 1992

The Chinese New Year starts on 4 February 1992. Until then the old year, the year of the Goat, is still making its presence felt.

The year of the Goat (15 February 1991–3 February 1992) will have been a reasonable year for the Rat. He will have made progress in many of his activities and impressed those around him with his considerable charm and abilities. Indeed, during the year he will undoubtedly have sown the seeds for further success, and the experience, skills, and knowledge he has gained will serve him extremely well in the year ahead.

The latter part of the year of the Goat will be a busy and possibly expensive time for the Rat. He will attend numerous social functions, and is likely to get together with friends he has not seen for a considerable while. However, if the Rat is able to take advantage of any opportunity to clear up outstanding matters and give some thought to his plans and priorities for the forthcoming year, he will find this time will be very usefully spent. He should also pay careful attention to any important correspondence that he receives in the closing stages of the year, as he could learn something that will be of great significance to him in the months ahead.

The year of the Monkey starts on 4 February 1992 and it will be a highly favourable year for the Rat. His hard work and efforts over the last few years will be rewarded, and he will find those around him will be more co-operative towards his ideas and plans. In his work he could be given additional and more rewarding responsibilities, and the prospects for a new job or promotion are especially favourable, particularly in the second half of the year.

There will, however, have been some Rats who have struggled over the last few years and have had difficulties to overcome, or who have felt that they have not been able to realize their true potential. This will change in 1992. All

Rats will notice an upturn in their fortunes, and the Rat should start the year in a positive and optimistic frame of mind and with a determination to do well. He should pursue the opportunities that he sees before him, and even if one or two may not work out as he had hoped, he should persevere. His accomplishments and achievements in 1992 will be well worth while.

Any Rat involved in education is also likely to make pleasing progress, and his results will amply compensate for any sacrifices that he might have had to make. Indeed, all Rats should take advantage of any opportunity they have to attend courses and increase their skills and knowledge. Academic matters are very favourably aspected for 1992.

The Rat will be much in demand with his family and friends over the year, and he will lead a most pleasant social life. For the single Rat romance is certainly in the air, and many will meet their future partner during the year, get engaged or married.

Naturally no year is without its problems, and any troubles that do occur for the Rat are likely to concern differences of opinion with those around him. When such problems do arise, the Rat should use his considerable skills to resolve the situation as quickly and amicably as he can. The one thing the Rat should try to avoid is being stubborn and intransigent. If he is, he could seriously strain his relations with others, and any resulting rifts or disagreements could take some time to sort out.

The Rat will be fortunate in financial matters over the year, and many will see a substantial improvement in their financial situation. Some Rats can also look forward to the fruition of an investment that they made some time ago, or to receiving a modest amount of money from an unexpected source. With the favourable trends that exist, the Rat should also consider entering some competitions over the year—luck is on his side!

Although the Rat is unlikely to travel far during 1992,

the journeys he does undertake are likely to be both pleasurable and most enjoyable. However, many Rats will prefer to spend much of their spare time doing jobs around the house or garden, and they will be delighted by what they are able to accomplish and the improvements they are able to make.

The Rat will enjoy reasonably good health during the year, although any Rat who is troubled by a particular complaint should not hesitate to seek medical advice, and should also make sure he follows the advice he is given, particularly where getting sufficient rest is concerned. Failure to do so could only prolong the problem and cause the Rat unnecessary discomfort.

Generally, however, the Rat will enjoy 1992 and be pleased with how his various activities develop. This is the year for being positive and bold, and with the right attitude and sufficient determination many Rats will secure the success and rewards they have been seeking these last few years.

As far as the different types of Rat are concerned 1992 will be a most significant year for the **Metal Rat**. He will make great strides in his work, and for those Metal Rats seeking employment or a change of career 1992 could present them with several opportunities which are ideally suited for them and which could also prove to be of considerable importance over the next few years. The Metal Rat will also lead a pleasant domestic and social life over the year. His family will be most supportive throughout 1992, and many Metal Rats can look forward to seeing an addition to their family or delighting in the achievements of a younger relation. An elderly person may, however, seek the Metal Rat's support and advice during the year, and any help that he is able to give will be more appreciated than the Metal Rat may realize at the time. Although the Metal Rat will have many demands on his time over the year, he will find it especially beneficial if he regularly sets some time aside to take part in some suitable sporting or recreational activity—he will feel noticeably better for doing so.

This will be an enjoyable year for the **Water Rat**. He will be much in demand with his family and friends and is likely to lead an active and pleasant social life. He will also do well in academic matters, and those Water Rats in work will impress those around them with their friendly and conscientious manner. However, despite the favourable trends that exist for him in the year of the Monkey, he should still keep his aims and aspirations to a realistic level and avoid committing himself to enterprises that he has neither the time nor inclination to complete. Trying to do too much at any one time or aiming for unrealistic objectives will only lead to disappointment and, throughout 1992, the Water Rat would do well to remember that 'a job worth doing is a job worth doing well or not at all.' If he bears this in mind his accomplishments during the year will be quite considerable and his reputation much enhanced. The Water Rat's interests will also give him much pleasure throughout the year—particularly any that allow him to use his creative skills in any way. Although he may have problems with some travel arrangements that he wants to make, his main holiday of the year will be most enjoyable and he will find that it will lead to several new and long-lasting friendships.

This will be a pleasant year for the **Wood Rat**. He can look forward to spending much of his spare time with his family and friends and also to attending several notable social functions. He will be generally lucky in financial matters over the year, although he should be wary about entering into any financial commitment without first checking all the facts and reading the small print. The Wood Rat will also derive much pleasure over the year from his hobbies and interests, and he could be approached to undertake some task or duty for which he is ideally suited and which will turn out to be both highly satisfying and most rewarding. Should the Wood Rat find himself with any awkward problems to sort out, he should not hesitate to seek the opinions of those around him—he will be helped by the advice he is given and also considerably heartened by the genuine affection that others hold him in.

This could be a highly pleasing and successful year for the **Fire Rat**, although much depends on his attitude and willingness to co-operate with others. The omens and trends for the Fire Rat are particularly favourable in 1992, but there is always a danger that he is tempted either to do too much single-handedly or to speak his mind too forcefully, thus impairing his relations with those around him. Provided the Fire Rat sets about his activities in his usual good-humoured and conscientious way, and provided he exercises restraint when dealing with any difficult or awkward problems, he can look forward to making a tremendous amount of progress. But as always, by being such a forceful character, much depends on his attitude and outlook. In his work the Fire Rat could be given additional responsibilities, and he is likely to be successful in financial matters. He will also greatly enjoy outdoor activities over the year—particularly gardening or walking, or just following a sport. The year also favours taking up a new interest and, again, if this enables the Fire Rat to get out of doors and gives him a break from his usual daytime activities, he is likely to find this pursuit both absorbing and also highly beneficial.

This will be a satisfying year for the **Earth Rat**. He will make considerable progress with many of his activities and will attain, or certainly go a long way towards attaining, one of his most cherished ambitions. This will be a year of progress and, with the trends looking so favourable, the Earth Rat should not hesitate to pursue the opportunities that he sees and promote himself and his talents. Others will look favourably on his ideas and he will find that he will be much in demand with colleagues, family and friends. He will be given new responsibilities in his work and will also be generally fortunate in financial matters.

However, while this will be a good year for the Earth Rat, he should nevertheless handle his relations with others with care, always taking into account their views and feelings. Also, if he senses any problems arising, he should do all in his power to sort them out before they escalate. However, if he sets about his activities with his usual good sense and in his caring and open manner, he will find that the esteem and respect others hold him in will greatly increase over the year, and this in turn will enhance his prospects for both this and future years.

**Action Plan for the Rat in 1992**
As a Rat you are most adept at spotting opportunities, and there will certainly be many opportunities for you in 1992. Indeed this will be a much improved year for you and you should set about your activities in your own determined and inimitable way. Be positive and determined and you are sure to do well. The only thing you really need to guard against is committing yourself to too many undertakings at any one time.

While those around you will be generally supportive and co-operative, you cannot afford to ignore the views and feelings of others. If you do, tension and problems are likely to occur and these could very easily mar what will otherwise be a very good year for you.

Keep a watchful eye over your finances. By being prudent and careful, you will notice a considerable improvement in your financial position over the year.

This will be a good year for you socially, and your circle of friends and acquaintances will steadily increase. If you have been lonely or are seeking friends, do try to go out more—you will certainly be glad you did. If you are unattached, 1992 is an excellent year for romance and meeting others.

# Famous Rats

Prince Karim Aga Khan, Alan Alda, Dave Allen, Ursula Andress, Louis Armstrong, Charles Aznavour, Irvin Berlin, Kenneth Branagh, Marlon Brando, Charlotte Brontë, George Bush, Lord Callaghan, Jimmy Carter, Pablo Casals, Raymond Chandler, Jack Charlton, Maurice Chevalier, Steve Cram, Barbara Dickson, Benjamin Disraeli, Elizabeth Dole, Noel Edmonds, T.S. Eliot, Ben Elton, Albert Finney, Sir Clement Freud, Clark Gable, Thomas Hardy, Haydn, Benny Hill, Roy Hudd, Glenda Jackson, Jean-Michel Jarre, Gene Kelly, F.W. de Klerk, Nastassja Kinski, Yves St Laurent, Lawrence of Arabia, Ivan Lendl, Gary Lineker, Andrew Lloyd Webber, Lulu, Earl Mountbatten, Olivia Newton-John, Richard Nixon, Robert Palmer, Captain Mark Phillips, Enoch Powell, the Queen Mother, Vanessa Redgrave, Burt Reynolds, Jonathan Ross, Prince, Ayrton Senna, William Shakespeare, Wayne Sleep, Tommy Steele, Shakin' Stevens, James Taylor, Leo Tolstoy, the Prince of Wales, Dennis Waterman, Kim Wilde, the Duke of York.

$$AB^2 + AC^2 = BC^2$$

# The Ox

| | | | |
|---|---|---|---|
| 19 February 1901 | to | 7 February 1902 | *Metal Ox* |
| 6 February 1913 | to | 25 January 1914 | *Water Ox* |
| 25 January 1925 | to | 12 February 1926 | *Wood Ox* |
| 11 February 1937 | to | 30 January 1938 | *Fire Ox* |
| 29 January 1949 | to | 16 February 1950 | *Earth Ox* |
| 15 February 1961 | to | 4 February 1962 | *Metal Ox* |
| 3 February 1973 | to | 22 January 1974 | *Water Ox* |
| 20 February 1985 | to | 8 February 1986 | *Wood Ox* |

## The Personality of the Ox

You have to believe in yourself, that's the secret.
*- Charlie Chaplin: an Ox.*

The Ox is born under the signs of equilibrium and tenacity. He is a hard and conscientious worker and sets about everything he does in a resolute, methodical and determined manner. He has considerable leadership qualities and is often admired for his tough and uncompromising nature. He knows what he wants to achieve in life and, as far as possible, will not be deflected from his ultimate objective.

The Ox takes his responsibilities and duties very seriously. He is decisive and quick to take advantage of any opportunity that comes his way. He is also sincere and places a great deal of trust in his friends and colleagues. He is nevertheless something of a loner. He is a quiet and private individual and often keeps his thoughts to himself. He also cherishes his independence and prefers to set about things in his own way rather than be bound by the dictates of others or be influenced by outside pressures.

The Ox tends to have a calm and tranquil nature, but if something angers him or he feels that someone has let him down he can have a fearsome temper. He can also be stubborn and obstinate and this can lead the Ox into conflict with others. Usually the Ox will succeed in getting his own way, but should things go against him, he is a poor loser and will take any defeat or setback extremely badly.

The Ox is often a deep thinker and rather studious. He is not particularly renowned for his sense of humour and does not take kindly to new gimmicks or anything too innovative. The Ox is too solid and traditional for that and he prefers to stick to the more conventional norm.

His home is very important to him and in some respects he treats it as a private sanctuary. His family tends to be closely knit and the Ox will make sure that each member does their fair share around the house. The Ox tends to be a hoarder, but he is always well-organized and neat. He also places great importance on punctuality and there is nothing that infuriates him more than to be kept waiting—particularly if it is due to someone else's inefficiency. The Ox can be a hard task master!

Once settled in a job or house the Ox will quite happily remain there for many years. He does not like change and he is also not particularly keen on travel. He does, however, enjoy gardening and other outdoor pursuits and he will often spend much of his spare time out of doors. The Ox is usually an excellent gardener and whenever possible he will always make sure he has a large area of ground to maintain. The Ox usually prefers to live in the country rather than the town.

Due to his dedicated and dependable nature, he will usually do well in his chosen career—providing he is given enough freedom to act on his own initiative. He invariably does well in politics, agriculture, and in careers which need specialized training. The Ox is also very gifted in the arts and there are many who have enjoyed considerable success as musicians or composers.

The Ox is not as outgoing as some and it often takes him a long time to establish friendships and feel relaxed in another person's company. His courtships are likely to be long, but once he is settled he will remain devoted and loyal to his partner. The Ox is particularly well-suited to those born under the signs of the Rat, Rabbit, Snake, and Rooster. He can also establish a good relationship with the Monkey, Dog, Pig, and another Ox, but he will find that he has little in common with the whimsical and sensitive Goat. He will also find it difficult to get on with the Horse, Dragon, and Tiger—the Ox prefers a quiet and peaceful existence and those born under these three signs tend to be a little too lively and impulsive for his liking.

The lady Ox has a kind and caring nature and her home and family are very much her pride and joy. She always tries to do her best for her partner and can be a most conscientious and loving partner. The lady Ox is an excellent organizer and she is also a very determined person and will often succeed in getting what she wants in life. She usually has a deep interest in the arts and is often a talented artist or musician.

The Ox is a very down-to-earth character. He is sincere, loyal and unpretentious. He can, however, be rather reserved and to some he may appear distant and aloof. He has a quiet nature, but underneath he is very strong-willed and ambitious. He has the courage of his convictions and is often prepared to stand up for what he believes is right, regardless of the consequences. He inspires confidence and trust and will rarely be short of people who are ready to support him or who admire his strong and resolute manner.

# The Five Different Types of Ox

In addition to the twelve signs of the Chinese zodiac, there are five elements, and these have a strengthening or moderating influence on the sign. The effects of the five elements on the Ox are described below, together with the years that the elements were exercising their influence. Therefore all Oxen born in 1901 and 1961 are Metal Oxen, those born in 1913 and 1973 are Water Oxen, and so on.

## Metal Ox: 1901, 1961
This Ox is confident and very strong-willed. He can be blunt and forthright in his views and is not afraid of speaking his mind. He sets about his objectives with a dogged determination, but he can become so wrapped up in his various activities that he can be oblivious to the thoughts and feelings of those around him, and this can sometimes be to his detriment. He is honest and dependable and will never promise more than he can deliver. He has a good appreciation of the arts and usually has a small circle of very good and loyal friends.

## Water Ox: 1913, 1973
This Ox has a sharp and penetrating mind. He is a good organizer and sets about his work in a methodical manner. He is not as narrow-minded as some of the other types of Oxen and is more willing to involve others in his plans and aspirations. He usually has very high moral standards and is often attracted to careers in public service. He is a good judge of character and has such a friendly and persuasive manner that he usually experiences little difficulty in securing his objectives. He is popular and has an excellent way with children.

## Wood Ox: 1925, 1985
The Wood Ox conducts himself with an air of dignity and authority and will often take a leading role in any enterprise with which he gets involved. He is very self-

confident and is direct in his dealings with others. He does, however, have a quick temper and has no hesitation in speaking his mind. He has tremendous drive and will-power and has an extremely good memory. The Wood Ox is particularly loyal and devoted to the members of his family and has a most caring nature.

**Fire Ox: 1937**
The Fire Ox has a powerful and assertive personality and is a hard and conscientious worker. He holds strong views and has very little patience when things do not go his own way. He can also get carried away in the excitement of the moment and does not always take into account the views of those around him. He nevertheless has many leadership qualities and will often reach positions of power, eminence, and wealth. He usually has a small group of loyal and close friends and is very devoted to his family.

**Earth Ox: 1949**
This Ox sets about everything he does in a sensible and level-headed manner. He is ambitious, but he is also realistic in his aims and is often prepared to work long hours in order to secure his objectives. He is shrewd in financial and business matters and is a very good judge of character. He has a quiet nature and is greatly admired for his sincerity and integrity. He is also very loyal to his family and friends and his views and opinions are often sought by others.

# Prospects for the Ox in 1992

The Chinese New Year starts on 4 February 1992. Until then the old year, the year of the Goat, is still making its presence felt.

The year of the Goat (15 February 1991–3 February 1992) will have been a varied year for the Ox. Although he will have enjoyed some successes, the year will also have been tinged with disappointments and a few awkward problems to overcome, especially where financial and property matters were concerned.

In addition, the Ox could have met with opposition from his colleagues and those around him, and might have found that some of his ideas and proposals were not as well received as he would have liked. However, despite any setbacks and disappointments the Ox may have experienced, the year of the Goat could still be seen as a constructive time for him, and the latter part of the year may mark the beginning of an upturn in his fortunes.

For what remains of the year of the Goat, the Ox should try to sort out any oustanding problems or difficulties that he has; with a concerted effort he will be pleased with what he can achieve at this time. The Christmas and New Year holidays will in any case be a most favourable time for the Ox, and as well as giving him the opportunity to be with his family and friends, it will also give him the chance to unwind and rest after the stresses of the year. He would do well to discuss his future plans with others and he will find some advice and information he is given will prove most useful for the year ahead.

The year of the Monkey starts on 4 February 1992 and it is going to be a significant year for the Ox. He will do well in most of his activities, and the year could bring with it a number of changes that will work out well for him. Admittedly the Ox is not one who particularly likes change and he may find some of the events that happen over the year a little unsettling, but he will be pleased with how the year develops and just how favourably events work out for him.

The Ox is likely to do particularly well in his work and, even if he has felt that his past efforts and achievements have been ignored, this has not been the case. Others have been watching the Ox with a growing admiration, and accordingly he is likely to be given new responsibilities, be promoted or moved to a different and more remunerative position over the course of year. Throughout the year the Ox should listen to the views of his colleagues and pay careful attention to all that is going on around him. He will find it advantageous to attend any courses that might be available to him and to use any opportunity to meet others who share similar views and interests. This is very much a year when the Ox will meet and impress others, and the contacts he is able to build up will prove of considerable importance to him in the months and years ahead.

Any Ox seeking employment is also likely to be fortunate in finding a suitable position and, again, if there is a course that he can go on that will give him an additional qualification or skill, this will certainly improve his prospects.

The Ox will be generally fortunate in financial matters over the year, and any Ox who may have been experiencing financial problems will find his situation eased during the year. Some Oxen may also be helped if they are able to take a part-time job or try to put one of their hobbies or interests to profitable use. With a little effort on their part, they will be surprised at what they can accomplish.

The Ox will have some most pleasant times with his family and friends over the year and many Oxen can look forward to being involved in a memorable family celebration or reunion. There will also be plenty of opportunities for the single Ox to meet with others in 1992, and the summer months in particular are likely to be a happy time.

The Ox will also derive much enjoyment over the year from outdoor pursuits, particularly from gardening or from being involved in some sporting activity. The Ox is also likely to enjoy any short journeys that he undertakes, and he will find that if he is able to take several breaks at different times of the year he will find this pleasurable and beneficial.

Generally this will be a good year for the Ox and he will make pleasing progress in many of his activities as well as leading an enjoyable social and domestic life. The main problems that are likely to arise over the year will mainly centre around any changes that take place—either in his work, social life or with his accommodation. These changes could give rise to a feeling of uncertainty and possibly insecurity, but the Ox should remember that he has others around him in whom he can confide; he will find that the support and advice he is given will be both helpful and reassuring. This will be an important year for him and it will also be a year many Oxen will be able to look back on with considerable satisfaction.

As far as the different types of Ox are concerned, 1992 will be an important year for the **Metal Ox**, as during the year he will be faced with several decisions concerning his long-term future. These decisions could involve a change in residence or job, and while the Metal Ox is usually very sure in his mind of what he wants, he should nevertheless spend time with others discussing the options available to him. He will be very gratified by the assistance and support others give him over the year. The one thing he should guard against in 1992 is making his mind up on the spur of the moment without fully considering the consequences or implications of his actions. With caution and his usual good sense, events will turn out well for him and he will be delighted with what he is able to achieve. He will also have some most enjoyable times with his family and friends over the year. Many Metal Oxen can look forward to a personal triumph in 1992 which will give rise to much celebration. With work, family and social commitments his spare time over the year will be limited, but he will nevertheless obtain much pleasure from one of his interests in 1992, and will find that this pursuit could develop in both a surprising and lucrative way. He will also build up some new and important friendships over the year.

The **Water Ox** will enjoy 1992. The year will present him with some splendid opportunities in which he can demonstrate his considerable skills and qualities. He will do well in his work, and any Water Ox involved in further education is likely to be pleased with his progress. Indeed the year is a highly favourable one for the Water Ox to add to his skills, and the knowledge and experience he gains during the year will serve him well in future. Those Water Oxen in work are likely to be given additional responsibilities over the year or will move to a completely different and more rewarding position; those seeking employment should pursue any opportunities that arise. With perseverance and determination their efforts will be rewarded. The Water Ox will lead a most enjoyable social life in 1992 and his circle of friends is likely to increase. He will be reasonably fortunate in financial matters, although he should still retain a certain amount of caution when dealing with his finances, taking care to avoid gambling or getting involved in risky ventures. By being prudent he will not go far wrong, but by taking risks he could all too easily end up the loser and considerably poorer. The Water Ox would do well to listen very closely to advice or information given by someone close to him as it could be more significant than he may at first realize.

This can be an enjoyable and pleasant year for the **Wood Ox**, although much does depend on his attitude and approach. Although the Wood Ox's inborn determination and resolute manner can be a very strong attribute, it can also sometimes lead him into conflict with others and involve him in complicated and occasionally awkward problems. In 1992 he should set about his various activities with a good heart, a willingness to listen to others and if need be to compromise. In this way he will find life much more pleasant, his progress greater and the year generally more enjoyable. Any Wood Ox who may have been lonely in recent years should make every attempt to go out more or perhaps join a local club or society—he will be very pleased he has made the effort and will soon find others who share his interests and tastes. Likewise if the Wood Ox would like to take up a new hobby, this would be an excellent year to do so—the year particularly favours artistic and creative pursuits such as music, writing, painting and photography. The Wood Ox will be generally fortunate in financial matters during 1992. He should also pay careful attention to any official correspondence he is sent, as it could contain some information which will prove of considerable importance to him in the future. The achievements of a younger relation in particular are likely to be a source of great pride and pleasure to him over the year.

This will be a successful year for the **Fire Ox**. He will do well in his various activities and have more time to devote to his family, interests and hobbies. He will also be generally fortunate in financial matters, although he should be wary about committing himself to any major financial undertaking or signing any legal document without first checking the small print. When in doubt he should not hesitate to seek professional advice. He will also find it helpful to conduct a review of his financial situation and make any necessary changes to his level of expenditure. He will be pleased with the results of his efforts. The Fire Ox will also be fortunate in some purchase that he makes over the year—especially items for his home or a collection that he is trying to build up. By keeping a look-out in the most unlikely of places he will spot some extremely good bargains over the year, some of which could prove to be worthy investments in years to come. Many Fire Oxen can also look forward to a family celebration in the year and to re-establishing contact with some friends and relations they have not seen for a long time.

This will be a year of steady progress for the **Earth Ox**. He will make considerable progress in his work, and some ideas or projects that he has been working on are likely to be well received. He will, however, have a generally heavy workload over the year, and it is essential that he allows himself the opportunity to relax and unwind, setting aside some time to be with his family and friends. With the many demands that will be made of the Earth Ox during the year, he will need to maintain a strict set of priorities. He should also remember that others are willing to help him should he need any additional support or advice. Although the Earth Ox will be relatively fortunate in financial matters over the year, he still needs to be careful with his expenditure. Many Earth Oxen will be tempted to have alterations carried out on their homes or gardens or will want to purchase expensive pieces of equipment. In all these cases the Earth Ox should get as many quotations as possible lest he gets involved in more expense than he anticipated. The Earth Ox will derive much pleasure and satisfaction from the achievements of someone close to him over the year, although he could also have a relative who has a dificult problem to overcome; any assistance he can give will be greatly appreciated and will do much to help.

## Action Plan for the Ox in 1992

As an Ox, stability and order in your life are very important to you. However 1992 is likely to be a year of change and, while this may be unsettling for you at the time, you will do extremely well as a result of these changes. It will be a favourable and significant year for you, and you should set about your activities in your own determined and tenacious way, welcoming changes as they occur as well as the opportunities they will undoubtedly bring.

Take advantage of any opportunity to advance your skills and widen your knowledge. The experience that you gain over the year will prove very important to you in the future.

With your many activities and demands on your time, do ensure that you take time to unwind and rest every now and again. Also, do remember that outdoor activities are

especially favourable for you over the year: you are likely
to derive considerable enjoyment from spending time in
your garden, from short journeys, and from visiting local
places of interest.

Involve others in your various activities and take
advantage of any opportunity to meet others, particularly
those who share your interests or who may yield influence
and authority. The friends, acquaintances and contacts
that you build up over the year will prove of great
significance to you both in this and the next few years.

# Famous Oxen

Johann Sebastian Bach, Richard Baker, Warren Beatty,
Menachem Begin, Tony Benn, Chuck Berry, Benjamin
Britten, Frank Bruno, Richard Burton, Barabara Bush, King
Carlos of Spain, Johnny Carson, Barbara Cartland, Judith
Chalmers, Charlie Chaplin, Peter Cook, Bill Cosby, Tony
Curtis, Sammy Davis Jr, Jacques Delors, Walt Disney, Anita
Dobson, Patrick Duffy, Jane Fonda, Michael Foot, Gerald
Ford, Peter Gabriel, Handel, Robert Hardy, Charles
Haughey, Nigel Havers, Adolf Hitler, Dustin Hoffman,
Anthony Hopkins, Billy Joel, Don Johnson, Jack Jones,
Mark Knopfler, Burt Lancaster, Jessica Lange, Angela
Lansbury, Jack Lemmon, Nicholas Lyndhurst, John
MacGregor, Barry McGuigan, David Mellor, Warren
Mitchell, Robert Mugabe, Napoleon, Pandit Nehru, Paul
Newman, Jack Nicholson, Kerry Packer, Oscar Peterson,
Robert Redford, Rubens, Ian Rush, Willie Rushton,
Richard Ryder, Arthur Scargill, Monica Seles, Peter Sellers,
Jean Sibelius, Valerie Singleton, Bruce Springsteen, Meryl
Streep, Margaret Thatcher, Twiggy, Mary Tyler Moore,
Dick Van Dyke, the Princess of Wales, the Duke of
Wellington, Alan Whicker, Ernie Wise, W.B. Yeats.

# The Tiger

| | | | |
|---|---|---|---|
| 8 February 1902 | to | 28 January 1903 | *Water Tiger* |
| 26 January 1914 | to | 13 February 1915 | *Wood Tiger* |
| 13 February 1926 | to | 1 February 1927 | *Fire Tiger* |
| 31 January 1938 | to | 18 February 1939 | *Earth Tiger* |
| 17 February 1950 | to | 5 February 1951 | *Metal Tiger* |
| 5 February 1962 | to | 24 January 1963 | *Water Tiger* |
| 23 January 1974 | to | 10 February 1975 | *Wood Tiger* |
| 9 February 1986 | to | 28 January 1987 | *Fire Tiger* |

## The Personality of the Tiger

Man, unlike any other thing organic or inorganic in the universe, grows beyond his work, walks up the stairs of his concepts, emerges ahead of his accomplishments.
— *John Steinbeck: a Tiger*.

The Tiger is born under the sign of courage. He is a charismatic figure and usually holds very firm views and beliefs.

He is strong-willed and determined and sets about most of the things he does with a tremendous energy and enthusiasm. He is very alert and quick-witted and his mind is forever active. He is a highly original thinker and is nearly always brimming with new ideas or is full of enthusiasm for some new project or scheme.

The Tiger adores challenges and he loves to get involved in anything which he thinks has an exciting future or which catches his imagination. He is prepared to take risks and does not like to be bound either by convention or the dictates of others. The Tiger likes to be free to act as he chooses and at least once during his life he will throw caution to the wind and go off and do the things he wants to do.

The Tiger does, however, have a somewhat restless nature. Even though he is often prepared to throw himself wholeheartedly into a project, his initial enthusiasm can soon wane if he sees something which offers more appeal. He can also be rather impulsive and there will have been occasions when he has acted in a manner which he has later regretted. If the Tiger were more prepared to think things out or to persevere in his various activities, he would almost certainly enjoy a greater degree of success than he would otherwise obtain.

Fortunately the Tiger is lucky in most of his enterprises, but should things not work out as he had hoped, he is liable to suffer from severe bouts of depression and it will often take him a long time to recover. The Tiger's life often consists of a series of ups and downs.

The Tiger is, however, very adaptable. He has an adventurous spirit and rarely stays in the same place for long. In the early stages of his life he is likely to try his hand at several different jobs and he will also change his residence fairly frequently.

The Tiger is very honest and open in his dealings with others. He hates any sort of hypocrisy or falsehood. He is also well known for being blunt and forthright and has no hesitation in speaking his mind. He can also be most rebellious at times—particularly against any form of petty authority—and while this can lead the Tiger into conflict with others, he is never one to shrink from an argument or not stand up for what he believes is right.

The Tiger is a natural leader and can invariably rise to the top of his chosen profession. He does not, however, care for anything too bureaucratic or detailed and he also does not like to obey orders. He can be stubborn and obstinate and throughout his life he likes to retain a certain amount of independence in his actions and be responsible to no one but himself. He likes to consider that all his achievements are due to his own efforts, and unless he cannot avoid it he will rarely ask for support from others.

Ironically, despite his self-confidence and leadership qualities, the Tiger can be indecisive and will often delay making a major decision until the very last moment. He can also be sensitive to criticism.

Although the Tiger is capable of earning large sums of money, he is rather a spendthrift and does not always put his money to its best use. He can also be most generous and will often shower lavish gifts on friends and relations.

The Tiger cares very much for his reputation and the image that he tries to project. He carries himself with an air of dignity and authority and enjoys being the centre of attention. He is very adept at attracting publicity, both for himself and for the causes which he supports.

The Tiger often marries young and he will find himself best suited to those born under the signs of the Pig, Dog, Horse and Goat. He can also get on well with the Rat, Rabbit, and Rooster, but the Tiger will find the Ox and Snake a bit too quiet and too serious for his liking and he will also get highly irritated with the Monkey's rather mischievous and inquisitive ways. The Tiger will also find it difficult to get on with another Tiger or a Dragon—both partners will want to dominate the relationship and could find it difficult to compromise on even the smallest of matters.

The Tigress is lively, witty and a marvellous hostess at parties. She is usually most attractive and takes great care over her appearance. She can also be a very doting mother, and, while she believes in letting her children have their freedom, she makes an excellent teacher and will ensure

that her children are brought up well and want for nothing.
Like her male counterpart, she has numerous interests and
likes to have sufficient independence and freedom to go
off and do the things that she wants to do. She also has a
most caring and generous nature.

The Tiger has many commendable qualities. He is
honest, courageous and is often a source of inspiration for
others. Providing he can curb the wilder excesses of his
restless nature, he is almost certain to lead a most fulfilling
and satisfying life.

# The Five Different Types of Tiger

In addition to the twelve signs of the Chinese zodiac, there
are five elements, and these have a strengthening or
moderating influence on the sign. The effects of the five
elements on the Tiger are described below, together with
the years that the elements were exercising their influence.
Therefore all Tigers born in 1950 are Metal Tigers, those
born in 1902 and 1962 are Water Tigers, and so on.

**Metal Tiger: 1950**
The Metal Tiger has an assertive and outgoing personality.
He is very ambitious and, while his aims may change from
time to time, he will work relentlessly until he has obtained
what he wants. He can, however, be impatient for results
and also get highly strung if things are not working out as
he would like. He is distinctive in his appearance and is
admired and respected by many.

**Water Tiger: 1902, 1962**
This Tiger has a wide variety of interests and is always
eager to experiment with new ideas or go off and explore
distant lands. He is versatile, shrewd, and has a kindly
nature. The Water Tiger tends to remain calm in a crisis,
although he can be annoyingly indecisive at times. He

communicates well with others and through his many capabilities and persuasive nature he usually achieves what he wants in life. He is also highly imaginative and is often a gifted orator or writer.

## Wood Tiger: 1914, 1974
The Wood Tiger has a very friendly and pleasant personality. He is less independent than some of the other types of Tiger and is more prepared to work with others to secure a desired objective. However, he does have a tendency to jump from one thing to another and can get easily distracted. He is usually very popular, has a large circle of friends, and invariably leads a busy and enjoyable social life. He also has a good sense of humour.

## Fire Tiger: 1926, 1986
The Fire Tiger sets about everything he does with great verve and enthusiasm. He loves action and is always ready to throw himself wholeheartedly into anything which catches his imagination. He has many leadership qualities and is capable of communicating his ideas and enthusiasm to others. He is very much an optimist and can be most generous. He has a likeable nature and can be a witty and persuasive speaker.

## Earth Tiger: 1938
This Tiger is responsible and level-headed. He studies everything objectively and tries to be scrupulously fair in all his dealings. Unlike other Tigers, he is prepared to specialize in certain areas rather than get distracted by other matters, but he can become so involved with what he is doing that he does not always take into account the views and opinions of those around him. He has good business sense and is usually very successful in later life. He has a large circle of friends and pays great attention to both his appearance and his reputation.

# Prospects for the Tiger in 1992

The Chinese New Year starts on 4 February 1992. Until then the old year, the year of the Goat, is still making its presence felt.

The year of the Goat (15 February 1991–3 February 1992) is likely to have been a mixed year for the Tiger. Although he will have enjoyed some successes, he could also have faced problems with some of the things that he had hoped to achieve, and may have found that others were not as co-operative or as receptive to his ideas as he would have liked. This could have proved very frustrating to the Tiger, who is usually so keen to achieve so much.

On a more positive note, the year of the Goat will have been a very good year for travel, and indeed many Tigers will have travelled considerable distances in the latter part of the year. Goat years are also generally good for business and financial matters and for carrying out home improvements. For those Tigers who still have modifications that they would like to carry out on their home, the latter part of the year of the Goat is a good time to carry these out. The Tiger is also likely to be particularly fortunate in some purchases that he makes both for himself and his home in the sales that follow Christmas.

The year of the Monkey starts on 4 February 1992 and it could be a tricky year for the Tiger. Despite all his zest, enthusiasm and his many ideas, the Tiger could find it difficult to achieve some of the aims and objectives he has set himself for the year. He could experience a number of delays and irritating problems over 1992, and it will generally take him longer to get things done than he would like. Although this may make disappointing reading for the Tiger, there are several things that he can do to help his situation. The first is to be diplomatic and tactful in his dealings with others—if not, he could inflame his relationships with those around him and exacerbate any situation that may already be difficult.

Another point that will help the Tiger is to concentrate on specific objectives rather than try to do too much at any one time. He should also resist the temptation of getting distracted by other matters over the year. He will find that he will get the best results by sticking to areas he knows rather than experimenting with new ideas. However, despite the variable trends that exist for the Tiger in 1992, he can nevertheless make pleasing progress in his work, and business affairs are well aspected. The Tiger will also be fortunate in financial matters, although it would be in his interests to exercise a certain amount of restraint in his spending, particularly if he is tempted to purchase any expensive item on the spur of the moment.

Those Tigers seeking employment should pursue any opportunity that comes their way or try to obtain a further skill or qualification. They will be pleased at how events turn out for them, but the success they desire will necessitate a lot of perseverance and determination on their part.

Travel is extremely well aspected in 1992, and many Tigers will go on some lengthy journeys which they will find most enjoyable. Likewise 1992 is a favourable year for any Tiger who wishes to widen his experience by working in another country. The opportunities for travelling are certainly there; it is up to the Tiger to seize any available opportunity.

The Tiger is likely to lead a busy social life over the year, and he can look forward to making some new and very good friends. However, domestic matters do need careful handling. He should listen to his loved ones and take into account their views and feelings. He should also make sure that he sets aside some time to be with them and share in their interests. If not, the Tiger could find tensions and misunderstandings developing—some of which are unnecessary and could easily have been avoided.

The Tiger will obtain much pleasure from his hobbies over the year. If he is able to get in contact with others who share his interests, or if he joins a society specializing in one of his pursuits, he will find this will further his interest a considerable amount and lead to new friendships and some enjoyable social occasions.

Although 1992 may not be the best of years for the Tiger, he will still enjoy some successes, particularly in work matters. Admittedly there will be delays and a number of small and niggling obstacles that he will have to overcome, but provided he remains patient (unfortunately not one of the Tiger's strong points!), persistent and diplomatic, he will be able to deal satisfactorily with any problems in his way, emerging with some worthy gains to his credit. He will also benefit immensely from the experience that he obtains over the year, and this will help further his prospects in the next few years.

As far as the different types of Tiger are concerned, 1992 will be both a significant and challenging year for the **Metal Tiger**. In some of his activities he will enjoy success, but in others the Metal Tiger will find his progress difficult and his plans frustrated. However his real gains will come through the ways he handles any problems that arise. By tackling these in a common-sense and rational manner, he will not only overcome the problems successfully but will win the admiration, respect and support of others, and this will be important to his future. However, if the Metal Tiger retains a rather independent stance and tackles problems in a heavy-handed manner, he could find his relationships with others becoming strained and the results that he seeks elusive. In 1992 he should remain diplomatic and set about his activities in a patient and steady manner. If he can do this, he will turn what could have been an awkward year into a year in which his reputation is considerably enhanced. Throughout the year the support that his family and friends give him will be most important, and he should not hesitate to share his hopes and aspirations for the future with them and to discuss any worries that he might have. He will be successful in financial matters, and towards the end of the year could obtain a new job or be given increased responsibilities in his work. He should also ensure that he gets away for at least one good holiday over the year—he will find this will prove most beneficial.

This will be a full and varied year for the **Water Tiger**. He can look forward to making progress in his work over the year, and is likely to be given new and increased responsibilities. However, he will be under a lot of pressure at various times during the year, and on these occasions he should not hesitate to ask others for assistance. Provided he organizes himself well and enlists the support of others when he needs it, he will be surprised at just how much he can accomplish—but he must remember, he cannot do everything single-handed. He is also likely to have increased responsibilities in his domestic life—either with an addition to his family or by being called upon to assist a relation or friend with a difficult problem. Throughout 1992 family matters need careful handling, but provided he is his usual considerate self and is prepared to compromise in any awkward situation, any difficulties or problems that do emerge will be short-lived. Although his spare time will be limited, he should ensure that he sets aside some time for recreational activities and also to travel when the opportunity arises. The Water Tiger will be fortunate in money matters, and any financial difficulties that he may have been experiencing will certainly ease during the year.

This will be a mixed year for the **Wood Tiger**, and while the year will contain some happy and enjoyable moments there will also be disappointments and a few problems to overcome. He could experience opposition to some of his plans and may have to revise or alter some of his objectives. However, most of the problems that he does have to face will be over within the first few months of the year and he can generally look forward to making progress, particularly in education or work matters. For any Wood Tiger seeking employment, he should not only pursue any opportunity that comes up but would also do well to investigate types of work he may not have considered before. By being adaptable and prepared to obtain as broad a range of experience as he can, he will do well. Throughout the year he should, however, pay careful attention to any advice he is given, particularly from those close to him and those who speak from experience. While he may not agree with everything he is told, there is much wisdom in their words and they advise with his best interests at heart. If he meets with any opposition to his plans he should listen to the views of others and if at all possible try to seek a compromise and amicable agreement. The Wood Tiger will also travel considerable distances over the year, and he can look forward to leading a busy social life and to making some new and good friends.

This is going to be an interesting but challenging year for the **Fire Tiger**. Provided he sets about his various activities in a calm, sensible manner and with the support of others he will enjoy considerable success. However if, as is sometimes the case, he lets his enthusiasm get the better of him and acts without thinking through the consequences of his action, he could create difficulties for himself. In 1992 he should guard against impulsive and rash acts, and as long as he does so he will find things will go well for him. He can look forward to some most pleasurable holidays and breaks during the year, and if he sees a hobby or new interest that intrigues him this could certainly be a good year to find out more about it. The Fire Tiger will also spend much time with his family and friends over the year, although at some time during 1992 he could be concerned about someone close to him—if this is the case he should not hesitate to offer any help and advice that he thinks necessary. He will be generally fortunate in financial matters and a long-term investment that he makes could turn out most favourably for him.

1992 is not going to be a particularly easy year for the **Earth Tiger**. There will have been many Earth Tigers who have become disenchanted with their work, disappointed by their lack of progress or just yearning for the opportunity to try something new. All the time this yearning for change is gnawing away at him, even though on the surface, the Earth Tiger may appear to give the impression that he is content with the way things are. However 1992 is not the year when he should make any major changes, at least not without first giving the matter considerable thought or acting without the backing and support of others. This is a year when he should avoid taking risks. Rather, he should look at 1992 more as a year for consolidating any gains that he may have made recently, and giving thought to his future. The ideas and plans that he comes up with will prove significant, but he should plan for the long-term rather than for 1992 itself. The Earth Tiger will, however, be generally fortunate in financial matters, and a savings policy or investment that he makes during the year could prove to be a very good asset in years to come. He will also have some pleasant times with his family, although he would do well to bear their views in mind, and pay careful attention to any advice he is given. The Earth Tiger will find that the year will improve for him as it goes on, and by dealing with his various activities in a cautious and guarded manner he will end the year in a more secure and content position, ready to take advantage of the better trends that lie ahead.

**Action Plan for the Tiger in 1992**
This can be a significant year for you, for while the year will not be without its problems, your achievements and accomplishments over the year will be worthwhile and will help prepare the way for future successes. Set about your activities with a determined spirit, bear in mind the views of others, and show yourself adaptable should you meet with any opposition to your plans.

Two of your best attributes are your resourcefulness and determination. Do remember these. If you experience any problems during the year, look for ways round the problem, regarding it as part of life's rich learning process. The experience you gain surmounting the problems that arise over the year will help strengthen and enrich your personality; this will be very important to your future progress.

Pay careful attention to the feelings and views of your family and those around you. Family matters need careful handling in 1992, and you will find it both helpful and beneficial to involve those around you in your various activities.

Travel is well aspected in 1992. Take advantage of any opportunity to travel over the year—you are likely to find your travels most enjoyable and rewarding for you.

## Famous Tigers

Sir David Attenborough, Queen Beatrix of the Netherlands, Beethoven, Jon Bon Jovi, Richard Branson, Isambard Kingdom Brunel, Simon Cadell, Tommy Cannon, Agatha Christie, James Clavell, David Coleman, Phil Collins, Alan Coren, Tom Cruise, Paul Daniels, Emily Dickinson, David Dimbleby, Isadora Duncan, Charles de Gaulle, Crystal Gayle, Goya, Sir Alec Guinness, Dwight Eisenhower, Frederick Forsyth, Bryan Gould, Evander Holyfield, Sir Geoffrey Howe, William Hurt, Derek Jacobi, David Jacobs, Caron Keating, Sara Kennedy, Stan Laurel, Ian McCaskill, Ramsay Macdonald, Karl Marx, Marilyn Monroe, Eric Morcambe, Sam Nunn, Rudolf Nureyev, Marco Polo, Suzi Quatro, the Queen, Lionel Ritchie, Diana Rigg, the Princess Royal, Sir Jimmy Saville, Phillip Schofield, Paganini, Jonathan Porrit, Sir David Steel, Pamela Stephenson, Dame Joan Sutherland, Dylan Thomas, Terry Wogan, Stevie Wonder.

# The Rabbit

| | | | |
|---|---|---|---|
| 29 January 1903 | to | 15 February 1904 | *Water Rabbit* |
| 14 February 1915 | to | 2 February 1916 | *Wood Rabbit* |
| 2 February 1927 | to | 22 January 1928 | *Fire Rabbit* |
| 19 February 1939 | to | 7 February 1940 | *Earth Rabbit* |
| 6 February 1951 | to | 26 January 1952 | *Metal Rabbit* |
| 25 January 1963 | to | 12 February 1964 | *Water Rabbit* |
| 11 February 1975 | to | 30 January 1976 | *Wood Rabbit* |
| 29 January 1987 | to | 16 February 1988 | *Fire Rabbit* |

## The Personality of the Rabbit

Our deeds still travel with us from afar,
And what we have been makes us what we are.
— *George Eliot: a Rabbit.*

The Rabbit is born under the signs of virtue and prudence. He is intelligent, well-mannered, and prefers a quiet and peaceful existence. He dislikes any sort of unpleasantness and will try to steer clear of arguments and disputes. He is very much a pacifist and tends to have a calming influence on those around him.

He has wide interests and usually has a good appreciation of the arts and the finer things in life. He also knows how to enjoy himself and will often gravitate to the best restaurants and night spots in town.

The Rabbit is a witty and intelligent speaker and loves being involved in a good discussion. His views and advice are often sought by others and he can be relied upon for being discreet and diplomatic. He will rarely raise his voice in anger and will even turn a blind eye to matters which displease him just to preserve the peace. The Rabbit likes to remain on good terms with everyone, but he can be rather sensitive and takes any form of criticism very badly. He will also be the first to get out of the way if he sees any form of trouble brewing.

The Rabbit is a quiet and efficient worker and has an extremely good memory. He is also very astute in business and financial matters, but his degree of success often depends on the conditions that prevail. He hates being in a situation which is fraught with tension or where he has to make quick and sudden decisions. Wherever possible he will plan his various activities with the utmost care and a good deal of caution. He does not like to take risks and does not take kindly to changes. Basically he seeks a secure, calm, and stable environment, and when conditions are right he is more than happy to leave things as they are.

The Rabbit is conscientious in most of the things that he does and, because of his methodical and ever-watchful nature, he can often do well in his chosen profession. He makes a good diplomat, lawyer, shopkeeper, administrator, or priest, and he excels in any job where he can use his superb skills as a communicator. He tends to be loyal to his employers and is respected for his integrity and honesty, but if the Rabbit ever finds himself in a position of great power he can become rather instransigent and authoritarian.

The Rabbit attaches great importance to his home and will often spend much time and money to maintain and furnish it and to fit it with all the latest comforts—the Rabbit is very much a creature of comfort! He is also something of a collector and there are many Rabbits who derive much pleasure from collecting antiques, stamps, coins, *objets d'art*, or anything else which catches their eye or particularly interests them.

The female Rabbit has a friendly, caring, and considerate nature and will do all in her power to give her home a happy and loving atmosphere. She is also very sociable and enjoys holding parties and entertaining. She has a great ability to make the maximum use of her time and, although she involves herself in numerous activities, she always manages to find time to sit back and enjoy a good read or a chat. She has a great sense of humour, is very artistic and is often a talented gardener.

The Rabbit takes considerable care over his appearance and is usually smart and very well turned out. He also attaches great importance to his relations with others and matters of the heart are particularly important to him. He will rarely be short of admirers and will often have several serious romances before he settles down. The Rabbit is not the most faithful of signs, but he will find that he is especially well-suited to those born under the signs of the Goat, Snake, Pig, and Ox. Due to his sociable and easygoing manner he can also get on well with the Tiger, Dragon, Horse, Monkey, Dog, and another Rabbit, but the Rabbit will feel ill-at-ease with the Rat and Rooster as both these signs tend to speak their mind and be critical in their comments—and the Rabbit just loathes any form of criticism or unpleasantness.

The Rabbit is usually lucky in life and often has the happy knack of being in the right place at the right time. He is talented and quick-witted, but he does sometimes put pleasure before work, and wherever possible will tend to opt for the easy life. He can at times be a little reserved and suspicious of the motives of others, but generally the Rabbit will lead a long and contented life and one which—as far as possible—will be free of strife and discord.

# The Five Different Types of Rabbit

In addition to the twelve signs of the Chinese zodiac, there are five elements, and these have a strengthening or moderating influence on the sign. The effects of the five elements on the Rabbit are described below, together with the years that the elements were exercising their influence. Therefore all Rabbits born in 1951 are Metal Rabbits, those born in 1903 and 1963 are Water Rabbits, and so on.

## Metal Rabbit: 1951
This Rabbit is capable, ambitious, and has very definite views on what he wants to achieve in life. He can occasionally appear reserved and aloof, but this is mainly because he likes to keep his thoughts and ideas to himself. He has a very quick and alert mind and is particularly shrewd in business matters. He can also be very cunning in his actions. The Metal Rabbit has a good appreciation of the arts and likes to mix in the best circles. He usually has a small but very loyal group of friends.

## Water Rabbit: 1903, 1963
The Water Rabbit is popular, intuitive, and keenly aware of the feelings of those around him. He can, however, be rather sensitive and tends to take things too much to heart. He is very precise and thorough in everything he does and has an exceedingly good memory. He tends to be quiet and at times rather withdrawn, but he expresses his ideas well and is highly regarded by his family, friends and colleagues.

## Wood Rabbit: 1915, 1987
The Wood Rabbit is likeable, easy going, and very adaptable. He prefers to work in groups rather than on his own and likes to have the support and encouragement of others. He can, however, be rather reticent in expressing

his views and it would be in his own interests if he could become a little more open and forthright and let others know how he felt on certain matters. He usually has many friends and enjoys an active social life. He is noted for his generosity.

### Fire Rabbit: 1927, 1987
The Fire Rabbit has a friendly outgoing personality. He likes socializing and being on good terms with everyone. He is discreet and diplomatic and has a very good understanding of human nature. He is also strong-willed, and provided he has the necessary backing and support he can go far in life. He does not, however, suffer adversity well and can become moody and depressed when things are not working out as he would like. The Fire Rabbit is very intuitive and there are some who are even noted for their psychic ability. He has a particularly good manner with children.

### Earth Rabbit: 1939
The Earth Rabbit is a quiet individual, but he is nevertheless very shrewd and astute. He is realistic in his aims and is prepared to work long and hard in order to achieve his objectives. He has good business sense and is invariably lucky in financial matters. He also has a very persuasive manner and usually experiences little difficulty in getting others to fall in with his plans. He is held in very high esteem by his friends and colleagues, and his views and opinions are often sought and highly valued.

## Prospects for the Rabbit in 1992

The Chinese New Year starts on 4 February 1992. Until then the old year, the year of the Goat, is still making its presence felt.

The year of the Goat (15 February 1991–3 February

1992) will have been a favourable year for the Rabbit. He is likely to have led an active social life, made some new friends and also attended some highly pleasurable social functions. Indeed, the latter part of the year of the Goat is an especially favourable time for the Rabbit socially, and even those Rabbits who may have felt lonely of late will find an improvement taking place in their social life and with it the opportunity to meet others.

The Rabbit will also have enjoyed success in many of his activities. Over the year he is likely to have been given additional responsibilities in his work or to have moved to another position, and he will undoubtedly have impressed those around him. Any Rabbit seeking employment should keep especially vigilant in the last few months of the year, as he could hear of some opportunities or receive some information that it would be very much in his interests to pursue.

The latter part of the Goat year could, however, prove an expensive time for the Rabbit, and he would do well to keep a watch on his level of expenditure and to exercise great care with any important correspondence, forms or agreements that he has to sign.

The year of the Monkey starts on 4 February 1992 and it will be a much quieter year for the Rabbit, a year when he will need to set about his activities in a rather cautious and guarded manner.

During the year, the Rabbit will be faced with a number of small and minor problems which, while not serious, could frustrate his progress and cause him to alter his plans. These problems could arise in almost any aspect of his life and might be brought about because information or correspondence that he is requiring does not arrive, because he has been misinformed about something or because others are hesitant about giving him their full support.

Admittedly this will be disappointing for the Rabbit, who so much likes to live an orderly and generally trouble-free existence, but despite these problems the Rabbit can still turn events to his advantage.

Should his plans be frustrated, he should look for ways round any problem and use his considerable persuasive powers to try and bring people round to his way of thinking. If he does not succeed, he should adopt a flexible and conciliatory manner, seeking a satisfactory solution or compromise to any conflict that has arisen. The one thing the Rabbit should not do is to ignore any problems in the hope that they will go away. This could only cause further delays and even make matters worse.

In his work the Rabbit will be able to consolidate any gains that he may recently have made and also make a modest amount of progress. However he should avoid taking risks in any of his undertakings, and should be wary of accepting information from unreliable sources. Provided he is cautious in all his business dealings, he will not go far wrong. He should also be careful in monetary matters, for while the Rabbit is usually most skilled when it comes to dealing with his finances, 1992 is not a year when he can afford to take risks.

On a more positive note, the Rabbit will continue to lead a very full and active social life over the year. He will be much in demand with his family and friends, and can look forward to attending some most enjoyable social gatherings. Romance is especially well aspected for the single Rabbit, and there are many who will meet their future partner over the year, or get engaged or married.

However, while social trends for the Rabbit are well aspected, domestic matters need careful handling and the Rabbit could well be called upon to help a close relation with a problem that he or she has. Any assistance, advice and support that the Rabbit can give will be greatly appreciated—probably more than he may realize at the time.

With the various demands and pressures on the Rabbit during the year, it is particularly essential that he allows

himself the opportunity to rest and unwind and to set aside
some time to devote to his own interests. Also, while he is
likely to enjoy good health over the year, if there is any
medical matter giving him concern he should not hesitate
to seek medical advice, no matter how small he may
consider the problem. It is better to be safe than sorry.

Generally the Rabbit will not fare badly during the year
provided he sets about his activities in his usual
conscientious and personable manner. But the moment he
takes risks—and particularly where money is concerned—
the Rabbit could find things going against him. This is very
much a year when he needs to be careful in his
undertakings and remain alert to all that is going on around
him. He should also make sure that he does not take any
major decision or action without the support of others.

As far as the different types of Rabbit are concerned,
1992 will be a reasonable year for the **Metal Rabbit**.
Fortunately he is very perceptive and a good judge of
character; this enables him to sense when the time is right
to act and also when to hold back from pursuing his
various aims and objectives. With the variable trends that
exist for the Rabbit in 1992, this skill could prove very
useful over the year. The Metal Rabbit should be his usual
diplomatic self when dealing with any awkward problems
that arise, and should be prepared to adjust to any change
in his situation. He will want to be particularly careful in
work matters and to avoid taking unnecessary risks or
making any major decision without very careful thought
and consideration. Admittedly this cautious attitude may
slow the Metal Rabbit down and prevent him from
securing all that he wants from the year, but he will
impress others and earn their respect, and this will prove
crucial to his progress and success over the next few years.
The Metal Rabbit may, however, experience a few
problems or pressures in his domestic life in 1992 that,
while not serious, he would do well to deal with as they
occur, remaining particularly attentive to the views and

feelings of those round him. He would also be helped if he let his family and friends become involved in his various interests and activities.

This will be a relatively quiet year for the **Water Rabbit**. He will make a modest amount of progress with his various activities and although not all the events of the year may go as well or be as trouble-free as he would like, he will still emerge from the year with some gains to his credit. Throughout the year he should listen to others and be wary of taking any action on his own or of maintaining an independent stance on anything. Likewise if he is faced with any difficult situation or is placed in a dilemma at any time over the year, he should not hesitate to seek the views and opinions of others—he will find this will be both helpful and reassuring. 1992 is very much a year when the Water Rabbit should act with others rather than on his own. His family responsibilities and various commitments will keep him fairly busy throughout the year. While there may well be times when he will despair over how he can get everything done, he will find others are willing to help and assist him, and this will do much to ease any pressure he may be under. The Water Rabbit will derive much satisfaction from one of his interests over the year, and if he has been tempted to take up a new interest or hobby this would be a good year to do so. He will also enjoy outdoor activities over the year, although if at any time he feels tired and lacking in energy, he will find a short break—or even just a brisk walk in the fresh air—will do much to revive his flagging spirits.

1992 will be a reasonable year for the **Wood Rabbit**. He can look forward to a particularly enjoyable social life and to having some good times with his friends and family. Romance is also well aspected and there will be plenty of opportunities to meet others and make new friends. However, despite the favourable social trends, the Wood Rabbit could have several awkward problems to overcome. He needs to be cautious in handling important paperwork and financial matters, and should avoid taking risks. He also needs to prove himself adaptable in his work and be prepared to listen to any advice he is given— particularly when it is given by those with experience. Likewise any Wood Rabbit seeking employment should again show himself to be adaptable and he should pursue any opportunity that he sees—with determination his efforts will certainly be rewarded. There will also be opportunities for the Wood Rabbit to travel over the year. While he will thoroughly enjoy the travelling that he does undertake, he should make sure that he sets aside a sufficient amount of money to cover his expenses and that he has sorted out his travel arrangements and documents before he leaves. If not, this could mar what would otherwise be a most enjoyable time away.

This will be a mixed year for the **Fire Rabbit**. Although the year will contain some very happy moments— particularly involving the achievements and success of some members of his family—the year will also contain a few awkward problems to deal with. These problems could occur in almost any aspect of his life, and while they could cause the Fire Rabbit some disappointment and worry at the time, as long as he is prepared to be flexible and conciliatory in his attitude, he will find the problems short-lived and readily overcome. If there are any matters giving him concern he should not hesitate to seek the advice and opinions of his family and colleagues, as he will find their comments and assistance both constructive and reassuring. Like all Rabbits, the Fire Rabbit needs to be especially careful in financial matters and must make sure that he understands the terms of any agreement he enters. A holiday taken in late summer will prove to be one of the best he has had for a long time and will do him a considerable amount of good.

This will be a challenging year for the **Earth Rabbit**. He could experience opposition to some of his plans over the year, or he may find that things do not always work out in the manner he had hoped. In all his activities the Earth Rabbit needs to remain continually aware of the views and feelings of others, and must be prepared to modify his plans should the need arise. The Earth Rabbit should also avoid taking any major risks or irrevocable action on the spur of the moment. Throughout the year he needs to remain vigilant and careful, and while some Earth Rabbits may find parts of the year frustrating, they will see that in time events will eventually turn to their advantage. This is very much a year for caution, patience and diplomacy. The Earth Rabbit can, however, look forward to a family celebration over the year—either a wedding or the birth of a grandchild—and he will also enjoy any travelling that he undertakes. Although his spare time will be somewhat limited, the Earth Rabbit would do well to set a specific time aside each week to devote to his own interests or to some activity unrelated to his usual occupation. He will find this will help him unwind from everyday pressures and will also be most beneficial and enjoyable for him.

## Action Plan for the Rabbit in 1992

As a Rabbit you are very fortunate in your ability to get on well with others and in that you have some very good friends on whom you can rely. Over the year, do remember these friends. In 1992 there will be some small and niggling problems that you will have to face and, while not serious, they could cause you some concern. Do discuss your concern and worries with others rather than keeping them to yourself. You will not only feel better for doing so, but those you consult will appreciate the trust that you place in them.

Be careful in money matters over the year and do not commit yourself to any large financial undertaking without checking the facts carefully. When in doubt it would be worth your seeking professional advice.

Make an effort to get your family and friends involved in your various activities. It is also important that you set aside some time to unwind every now and again. If possible, take up a new hobby, one totally unrelated to your daytime activities. You will feel much better for doing so.

Socially 1992 will be a very pleasant year for you, and if you would like to lead a fuller and more active social life, do consider joining a local club or society or getting in contact with those who share your interests. You could build up some very good friends over the year.

Keep alert for new opportunities, especially where work is concerned, and give some thought to your longer term future. Some ideas that you come up with will prove very significant over the next few years.

## Famous Rabbits

Prince Albert, Cecil Beaton, Harry Belafonte, Ingrid Bergman, Melvyn Bragg, Lewis Carroll, Fidel Castro, John Cleese, Confucius, Kenny Dalglish, Peter Davison, Ken Dodd, Val Doonican, Paul Eddington, Albert Einstein, Peter Falk, W.C. Fields, Jodie Foster, James Fox, Jan Francis, David Frost, James Galway, Zina Garrison, Cary Grant, John Gummer, Sir Richard Hadlee, Oliver Hardy, Bob Hope, Whitney Houston, John Hurt, Clive James, David Jason, Gary Kasparov, Penelope Keith, Patrick Lichfield, Ali MacGraw, George Michael, Roger Moore, Malcolm Muggeridge, Brian Mulroney, Nanette Newman, King Olav V of Norway, George Orwell, John Peel, Eva Peron, Edith Piaf, Denis Quilley, Andrew Ridgeley, Ken Russell, Elizabeth Schwarzkopf, George C. Scott, Selina Scott, Terry Scott, Sir Walter Scott, Neil Sedaka, George

Simenon, Neil Simon, Frank Sinatra, Dusty Springfield, Sting, Jimmy Tarbuck, Denis Thatcher, J.R.R. Tolkien, Arturo Toscanini, Liv Ullman, Luther Vandross, Queen Victoria, Terry Waite, Orson Welles.

# The Dragon

| | | | |
|---|---|---|---|
| 16 February 1904 | to | 3 February 1905 | *Wood Dragon* |
| 3 February 1916 | to | 22 January 1917 | *Fire Dragon* |
| 23 January 1928 | to | 9 February 1929 | *Earth Dragon* |
| 8 February 1940 | to | 26 January 1941 | *Metal Dragon* |
| 27 January 1952 | to | 13 February 1953 | *Water Dragon* |
| 13 February 1964 | to | 1 February 1965 | *Wood Dragon* |
| 31 January 1976 | to | 17 February 1977 | *Fire Dragon* |
| 17 February 1988 | to | 5 February 1989 | *Earth Dragon* |

## The Personality of the Dragon

I ought, therefore I can.
*– Attributed to Immanuel Keat: a Dragon.*

The Dragon is born under the sign of luck. He is a proud and lively character and has a tremendous amount of self-confidence. He is also highly intelligent and very quick to take advantage of any opportunities that occur. He is ambitious and determined and will do well in practically anything which he attempts. He is also something of a perfectionist and will always try and maintain the high standards which he sets himself.

The Dragon does not suffer fools gladly and will be quick to criticize anyone or anything that displeases him. He can be blunt and forthright in his views and is certainly not renowned for being either tactful or diplomatic. He does, however, often take people at their word and can occasionally be rather gullible. If he ever feels that his trust has been abused or his dignity wounded he can sometimes become very bitter and it will take him a long time to forgive and forget.

The Dragon is usually very outgoing and is particularly adept at attracting attention and publicity. He enjoys being in the limelight and is often at his best when he is confronted by a difficult problem or tense situation. In some respects he is a showman and he rarely lacks for an audience. His views and opinions are very highly valued and he invariably has something interesting—and sometimes controversial—to say.

He has considerable energy and is often prepared to work long and unsocial hours in order to achieve what he wants. He can, however, be rather impulsive and does not always consider the consequences of his actions. He also has a tendency to live for the moment, and there is nothing that riles him more than to be kept waiting. The Dragon hates delays and can get extremely impatient and irritable over even the smallest of hold-ups.

The Dragon has an enormous faith in his abilities, but he does run the risk of becoming over-confident and unless he is careful can sometimes make grave errors of judgement. While this may prove disastrous at the time, he does have the tenacity and ability to bounce back and pick up the pieces again.

The Dragon has such an assertive personality, so much will-power, and such a desire to succeed that he will often reach the top of his chosen profession. He has considerable leadership qualities and will do well in positions where he can put his own ideas and policies into practice. He is usually successful in politics, showbusiness, as the manager of his own department or business, and in any job which brings him into contact with the media.

The Dragon relies a tremendous amount on his own judgement and can be scornful of other people's advice. He likes to feel self-sufficient, and there are many Dragons who cherish their independence to such a degree that they prefer to remain single throughout their lives. However, the Dragon will often have numerous admirers and there are many who are attracted by his flamboyant personality and striking looks. If he does marry, he will usually marry young and will find himself particularly well-suited to those born under the signs of the Snake, Rat, Monkey, and Rooster. He will also find the Rabbit, Pig, Horse, and Goat make ideal companions and will readily join in with many of his escapades. Two Dragons will also get on well together as they understand each other, but the Dragon may not find things so easy with the Ox and the Dog as both will be critical of his impulsive and somewhat extrovert manner. He will also find it difficult to form an alliance with the Tiger, for the Tiger—like the Dragon—tends to speak his mind, is very strong willed, and likes to take the lead.

The female Dragon knows what she wants in life and sets about everything she does in a very determined and positive manner. No job is too small for her and she is often prepared to work extremely hard until she has secured her objective. She is immensely practical and somewhat liberated. She hates being bound by routine and petty restrictions and likes to have sufficient freedom to be able to go off and do what she wants to do. Like her male counterpart, she also has a tendency to speak her mind.

The Dragon usually has many interests and enjoys sport and other outdoor activities. He has a very adventurous streak in him and providing his financial circumstances permit—and the Dragon is usually sensible with his money—he will travel considerable distances during his lifetime.

The Dragon is a very flamboyant character and, while he can be demanding of others and in his early years rather precocious, he will have many friends and will nearly always be the centre of attention. He has charisma and so much confidence in himself that he can often become a source of inspiration for others. In China he is the leader of the carnival and he is also blessed with an inordinate share of luck.

# The Five Different Types of Dragon

In addition to the twelve signs of the Chinese zodiac, there are five elements, and these have a strengthening or moderating influence on the sign. The effects of the five elements on the Dragon are described below, together with the years that the elements were exercising their influence. Therefore all Dragons born in 1940 are Metal Dragons, those born in 1892 and 1952 are Water Dragons, and so on.

## Metal Dragon: 1940
This Dragon is very strong-willed and has a particularly forceful personality. He is energetic, ambitious, and tries to be scrupulous in his dealings with others. He can also be blunt and to the point and usually has no hesitation in speaking his mind. If people disagree with him, or are not prepared to co-operate, he is more than happy to go his own way. The Metal Dragon usually has very high moral values and he is highly regarded by his friends and colleagues.

## Water Dragon: 1892, 1952
This Dragon is friendly, easy-going and intelligent. He is quick-witted and rarely lets an opportunity slip by. However, he is not as impatient as some of the other types of Dragons and is more prepared to wait for results rather than expect everything to happen that moment. He has an understanding nature and is prepared to share his ideas and

co-operate with others. His main failing, though, is a tendency to jump from one thing to another rather than concentrate on the job in hand. He has a good sense of humour and is an effective speaker.

## Wood Dragon: 1904, 1964
The Wood Dragon is practical, imaginative, and inquisitive. He loves delving into all manner of subjects and can quite often come up with some highly original ideas. He is a thinker and a doer and he has sufficient drive and commitment to put many of his ideas into practice. He is more diplomatic than some of the other types of Dragon and has a good sense of humour. He is very astute in business matters and can also be most generous.

## Fire Dragon: 1916, 1976
This Dragon is ambitious, articulate, and has a tremendous desire to succeed. He is a hard and conscientious worker and is often admired for his integrity and forthright nature. He is very strong willed and has considerable leadership qualities. He can, however, rely a bit too much on his own judgement and not take into account the views and feelings of others. He can also be rather aloof and it would certainly be in his own interests to let others join in more with his various activities. The Fire Dragon usually gets much enjoyment from music, literature and the arts.

## Earth Dragon: 1928, 1988
The Earth Dragon tends to be quieter and more reflective than some of the other types of Dragon. He has a wide variety of interests and is keenly aware of what is going on around him. He also has clear objectives and usually has no problems in obtaining support and backing for any of his ventures. He is a good organizer, mixes well with others, and usually has a large circle of friends.

# Prospects for the Dragon in 1992

The Chinese New Year starts on 4 February 1992. Until then the old year, the year of the Goat, is still making its presence felt.

The year of the Goat (15 February 1991–3 February 1992) is likely to have been a reasonably good year for the Dragon. However, although he will have enjoyed some success and made a modest amount of progress with many of his activities, not everything will have gone his way. He could have experienced opposition to some of his plans and found that others were not as co-operative as he would have liked. Indeed, in all his personal dealings the Dragon needs to be careful and tactful, and this certainly applies to the closing stages of the year of the Goat.

With the improved trends that will appear in the New Year, the Dragon cannot afford to sour his relationships needlessly. If there is anything that he can do to sort out remaining differences of opinion or heal old wounds, the closing stages of the Goat year would be an excellent time to do this.

The Dragon needs to be especially careful in financial matters and to avoid the temptation to gamble or become involved in anything risky or highly speculative. The year of the Goat is just not the right year to take any monetary risks—he could easily end up the loser.

The Dragon will, however, enjoy Christmas and the New Year holidays, and they will provide him with the time to rest and unwind after the exertions of the year. Although he may not have noticed it, the pressures of the year will have taken a lot out of him and the holiday period will offer an ideal opportunity time to rest, prepare for the New Year and be with his family and friends.

The year of the Monkey starts on 4 February 1992 and it is going to be a most interesting year for the Dragon. If in recent years he has felt hampered by a lack of support for his plans or felt that he has not made as much progress as he would have liked, this will now change. Very early on in the year the Dragon will notice a subtle change coming over him—he will begin to feel more determined and better able to overcome past difficulties and setbacks. He will feel imbued with a stronger spirit of determination and a desire to realize his full potential, and in most of his activities the Dragon can look forward to making a substantial amount of progress.

He will do well in his work and he should lose no opportunity to promote his own ideas or to pursue any opportunity that comes his way. If it is a new job or promotion he is seeking, his efforts will be rewarded. But here lies a warning. Throughout the year the Dragon cannot afford to be complacent or lulled into a false sense of security. He must not take liberties or risks, otherwise his success could be snatched from him. He should remember that this is the year of the Monkey, and that while the Monkey is usually happy for him to do well and prosper, he could still, with his great sense of mischief, place a few obstacles or difficulties in the way. The Dragon needs to remain watchful and alert lest he fall into any of the Monkey's traps.

While work matters are favourably aspected, the Dragon needs to exercise care in all his financial undertakings. As with 1991, this is not a year when he can afford to take risks with his money. Even if the Dragon should find himself in a relatively secure and stable financial situation, it is still necessary for him to keep a watchful eye over his level of spending and be careful before parting with any large sum of money. If he intends to make any significant purchase over the year the Dragon would do well to look around and compare prices, otherwise he could easily find himself involved in more expense than is necessary.

The Dragon is unlikely to travel far during the year but the journeys that he does undertake are likely to be most pleasurable. Indeed, rather than travel great distances many Dragons will be content to spend much of their spare time at home or visiting local places of interest; they are likely to find these pursuits most enjoyable.

The Dragon will lead an active social life over the year, although he could experience a few tensions in his domestic life. These are unlikely to be serious and could be caused by his proccupation with his own activities or, in the case of a difference of opinion, by his intransigency and unwillingness to take the views of others into account. If he does find himself in such a situation and notices a souring in his relationships, he should make every attempt to sort out the differences and, if need be, swallow his Dragon pride and seek a compromise. To do otherwise could only make his dealings with those around him even more difficult and cause him worry and unhappiness—much of which is unnecessary and avoidable.

Generally, however, the Dragon will have cause to remember 1992 with much satisfaction. He is likely to do well in most of his activities, and providing he does not become complacent in his work and handles financial matters and personal relationships with care, this will be a relatively successful year for him. In addition, the progress he makes over the year will help to prepare him for the major advances he will make in 1993, a truly auspicious Rooster year for him.

As far as the different types of Dragon are concerned, the **Metal Dragon** will find 1992 an interesting and varied year. Although his activities will generally go well, some of his plans could be changed by a series of unexpected events. While these could cause the Metal Dragon some concern and worry at the time, events will eventually move very much in his favour. In 1992 he should show himself to be adaptable, willing to adjust to new situations and ready to accommodate the views of others. If he can do this, his gains over the year will be very considerable. Like all Dragons, the Metal Dragon needs to be careful with his finances and should make sure that he understands the full implications of any large transaction he is about to enter into. The Metal Dragon should also give some thought to his long-term future, and would do well to discuss his aspirations with his family and those around him. The plans and ideas that he draws up will prove most important and will have far-reaching consequences. Indeed the Metal Dragon would do well to consider 1992 as a year for planning, leaving 1993 to be the year when these plans are put into practice. Although his spare time will be limited, his various hobbies and interests will give him much satisfaction over the year, and a particular skill or interest could turn out to be quite lucrative for him.

The **Water Dragon** can look forward to making considerable progress over the year. He is likely to do very well in his work, and many Water Dragons will be successful in their pursuit of a new and more rewarding position. Despite this, the Water Dragon cannot afford to take risks or automatically assume that he has the support of others. Throughout the year he will need to work hard and a moment of carelessness or complacency or an ill-timed comment could easily rebound on him. The amount of success that he enjoys over the year—and it could be quite considerable—depends a lot on his determination and his careful handling of others. He could also find that family and domestic matters will take up much of his spare time, and although some of these matters could cause him concern, he should not hesitate to discuss his feelings and any worries that he might have with others. Also, in the interests of domestic harmony he should let others be involved in all his plans and activities, as well as taking an active interest in all that is going on around him. By doing this and by adopting an open and caring attitude he will find the bonds between himself and those close to him are strengthened. Many Water Dragons are likely to carry out extensive work on their garden or home over the year and, while they will be pleased with the finished result, the work could prove more time consuming and expensive than they anticipated. The Water Dragon will thoroughly enjoy several short breaks that he goes on over the year and one, arranged at very short notice, will prove especially memorable.

This will be a highly favourable year for the **Wood Dragon**. He will make considerable progress in his work and could be offered a new job or promotion and a sizeable increase in salary. He will also find others more amenable to his ideas and plans. He should not hesitate to seize any opportunity to put forward ideas or suggestions that he has or to pursue his own objectives. Others will be greatly impressed by his conscientious and commanding manner, and over the year he will win the respect and admiration of many people; this will help his future prospects enormously. However, although there are many favourable trends for the Wood Dragon in 1992, he should remain careful and alert to all that is going on around him, particularly when dealing with important paperwork or official forms. A mistake or oversight could cause him numerous problems. His family responsibilities and various commitments will also take up much of his spare time, and like all Dragons, the Wood Dragon needs to be particularly attentive to the views and feelings of his family if he wishes to preserve domestic harmony. The achievements of a younger relation will give him much joy, and he would do well to bear in mind the advice that an elderly relative or friend gives him over the year, no matter how unorthodox or surprising it might be. There will be much wisdom in these words.

This will be a generally enjoyable and successful year for the **Fire Dragon**, although he will still need to set about his activities with a certain amount of care. He should guard against making any major decision or taking any important action without giving the matter serious thought, and throughout the year he should bear in mind the views and feelings of the members of his family and those around him. Although he may not agree with or fully appreciate all the advice they give, he should remember that they have his interests at heart and want to see his future successful and happy. The Fire Dragon should also be wary of committing himself to too many activities at any one time—he does have a tendency to be overambitious, and too many commitments or distractions could limit the amount of success he would otherwise enjoy. He will however lead a most pleasant social life over the year, making some new and very good friends. He will also find outdoor activities particularly enjoyable over the year, and a new interest that he takes up—such as photography, painting, music or some other creative activity—is likely to be a source of great pleasure to him.

This will be a pleasant year for the **Earth Dragon**. He can look forward to making progress in many of his activities, having the time to devote to his various interests, and also leading a pleasant social life. However, despite the generally good trends for the Earth Dragon, he could still encounter problems with some of the plans that he hopes to carry out. Throughout 1992 he would do well continually to bear in mind the views of others and to keep a close watch on all that is going on around him. In case of opposition to any of his plans, he should show himself conciliatory, flexible and ready to compromise—this way his gains will be considerably greater than if he remained intransigent and steadfastly committed to one point of view. The Earth Dragon will, however, be generally fortunate in financial matters in 1992—many could receive a small windfall over the year. Despite any good fortune that he enjoys, the Earth Dragon should be wary of being lulled into a false sense of security, and should exercise great care when making any large purchase or entering into any major financial agreement. Failure to do so could leave him committed to more expense than he originally anticipated. The Earth Dragon will, however, lead a most pleasant social life over the year, and many can look forward to making some new and very good friends. He is also likely to meet or re-establish contact with some friends or relations that he has not seen for a long time, and this will give him a considerable amount of pleasure and joy.

## Action Plan for the Dragon in 1992

There will be plenty of opportunities for you this year and you can look forward to making progress in many of your activities. However, over the year you will need to show restraint and curb your impulsive nature. An action taken on the spur of the moment could easily undo all the good things you have accomplished, and in this, the year of the Monkey, you must avoid doing anything that you could later regret. If you bear this in mind, 1992 will be a good and prosperous year for you.

Do not take any major decision or irrevocable action without first considering all the consequences. Where possible seek the advice and support of others. If you act hastily and independently you could find yourself isolated, and this could prove to be a limiting factor on your progress and ultimate success over the year.

Make sure that you spend time with your family and friends, and try to avoid becoming too preoccupied with your own activities at the expense of your personal relationships. Try to spread your activities out and involve those around you in the things that you do.

Handle money matters with care, and avoid being too extravagant with any spare money that you might have. This could prove very useful to you later.

## Famous Dragons

Jenny Agutter, Moira Anderson, Jeffrey Archer, Joan Baez, Peter Barkworth, Roseanne Barr, Count Basie, St Berna-

dette, Geoff Boycott, Tim Brooke-Taylor, Sir Alastair
Burnet, Jennifer Capriati, Neneh Cherry, Kenneth Clarke,
James Coburn, Bing Crosby, Roald Dahl, Salvador Dali,
Matt Dillon, Neil Diamond, Placido Domingo, Faye
Dunaway, Prince Edward, Bruce Forsyth, Michael
Gambon, Sir John Gielgud, Graham Greene, Chu Guevara,
Edward Heath, James Herriot, Gloria Hunniford, Joan of
Arc, Tom Jones, Martin Luther King, Ian Lang, Bonnie
Langford, John Lennon, Queen Margrethe II of Denmark,
Yehudi Menuhin, François Mitterand, Bob Monkhouse,
Desmond Morris, Johnny Morris, Hosni Mubarak, Florence
Nightingale, Elaine Paige, Gregory Peck, Richard Pryor,
Esther Rantzen, Christopher Reeve, Cliff Richard, George
Bernard Shaw, Eduard Shevardnadze, Mel Smith, Ringo
Starr, Princess Stephanie of Monaco, Karlheinz
Stockhausen, Shirley Temple, Christopher Timothy, Lord
(Harold) Wilson of Rievaulx.

# The Snake

| | | |
|---|---|---|
| 4 February 1905 to | 24 January 1906 | *Wood Snake* |
| 23 January 1917 to | 10 February 1918 | *Fire Snake* |
| 10 February 1929 to | 29 January 1930 | *Earth Snake* |
| 27 January 1941 to | 14 February 1942 | *Metal Snake* |
| 14 February 1953 to | 2 February 1954 | *Water Snake* |
| 2 February 1965 to | 20 January 1966 | *Wood Snake* |
| 18 February 1977 to | 6 February 1978 | *Fire Snake* |
| 6 February 1989 to | 26 January 1990 | *Earth Snake* |

## The Personality of the Snake

Character, in great and little things, means carrying
through what you feel able to do.
—*Johann Wolfgang von Goethe: a Snake.*

The Snake is born under the sign of wisdom. He is highly
intelligent and his mind is forever active. He is always
planning and always looking for ways in which he can use
his considerable skills. He is a deep thinker and likes to
meditate and reflect.

Many times during his life he will shed one of his famous
Snake skins and take up new interests or start a completely
different job. The Snake enjoys a challenge, and he rarely
makes mistakes. He is a skilful organizer, has considerable

business acumen, and is usually lucky in money matters. Most Snakes are financially secure in their later years, provided they do not gamble—the Snake has the distinction of being the worst gambler in the whole of the Chinese zodiac!

The Snake generally has a calm and placid nature and prefers the quieter things in life. He does not like to be in a frenzied atmosphere and hates being hurried into making a quick decision. He also does not like interference in his affairs and tends to rely on his own judgement rather than listen to advice.

The Snake can at times appear solitary. He is quiet, reserved, and sometimes has difficulty in communicating with others. He has little time for idle gossip and will certainly not suffer fools gladly. He does, however, have a good sense of humour, and this is particularly appreciated in times of crisis.

The Snake is certainly not afraid of hard work and is thorough in all that he does. He is very determined and can occasionally be ruthless in order to achieve his aims. His confidence, will-power and quick thinking usually ensure his success, but should he fail it will often take a long time for him to recover. He cannot bear failure and is a very bad loser.

The Snake can also be evasive and does not willingly let people into his confidence. This secrecy and distrust can sometimes work against him, and it is a trait which all Snakes should try to overcome.

Another characteristic of the Snake is his tendency to rest after any sudden or prolonged bout of activity. He burns up so much nervous energy that without proper care he can—if he is not careful—be susceptible to high blood pressure and nervous disorders.

It has sometimes been said that the Snake is a late starter in life and this is mainly because it often takes him a while to find a job with which he is genuinely happy. However, the Snake will usually do well in any position which involves research and writing and where he is given sufficient freedom to develop his own ideas and plans. He makes a good teacher, politician, personnel manager, and social adviser.

The Snake chooses his friends carefully, and while he keeps a tight control over his finances he can be particularly generous to those he likes. He will think nothing of buying expensive gifts or treating his friends or loved ones to the best theatre seats in town. In return he demands loyalty. The Snake is very possessive and he can get extremely jealous and hurt if he finds his trust has been abused.

The Snake is also renowned for his good looks and is never short of admirers. The female Snake in particular is most alluring. She has style, grace, and excellent (and usually expensive) taste in clothes. A keen socializer, she is likely to have a wide range of friends and has a happy knack of impressing those who matter. She has numerous interests and her advice and opinions are often highly valued. She is generally a calm-natured person and, while she involves herself in many activities, she likes to retain a certain amount of privacy in the things that she does.

The affairs of the heart are very important to the Snake and he will often have many romances before he finally settles down. He will find that he is particularly well suited to those born under the signs of the Ox, Dragon, Rabbit and Rooster. Provided the Snake is allowed sufficient freedom to pursue his own interests he can also build up a very satisfactory relationship with the Rat, Horse, Goat, Monkey and Dog, but he should try to steer clear of another Snake as they could very easily become jealous of each other. The Snake will also have difficulty in getting on with the honest and down-to-earth Pig, and will find the Tiger far too much of a disruptive influence on his quiet and peace-loving ways.

The Snake certainly appreciates the finer things in life. He enjoys good food and often takes a keen interest in the arts. He also enjoys reading and is invariably drawn to subjects such as philosophy, political thought, religion, or the occult. He is fascinated by the unknown and his enquiring mind is always looking for answers. Some of the world's most original thinkers have been Snakes, and— although they may not readily admit it—the Snake is often psychic and relies a lot on intuition.

The Snake is certainly not the most energetic member of the Chinese zodiac. He prefers to proceed at his own pace and to do the things he wants. He is very much his own master and throughout his life he will try his hand at many things. The Snake is something of a dabbler, but at some time—and usually when he least expects it—his hard work and his efforts will be recognized and he will invariably meet with the success and the financial security which he so much desires.

# The Five Different Types of Snake

In addition to the twelve signs of the Chinese zodiac, there are five elements, and these have a strengthening or moderating influence on the sign. The effects of the five elements on the Snake are described below, together with the years that the elements were exercising their influence. Therefore all Snakes born in 1941 are Metal Snakes, those born in 1893 and 1953 are Water Snakes, and so on.

**Metal Snake: 1941**
This Snake is quiet, confident and fiercely independent. He often prefers to work on his own and will only let a privileged few into his confidence. He is quick to spot opportunities and will set about achieving his objectives with an awesome determination. He is astute in financial matters and will often invest his money well. He also has a liking for the finer things in life and has a good appreciation of the arts, literature, music and good food.

He usually has a small group of extremely good friends and can be generous to his loved ones.

## Water Snake: 1893, 1953
This Snake has a wide variety of interests. He enjoys studying all manner of subjects and is capable of undertaking quite detailed research and becoming a specialist in his chosen area. He is highly intelligent, has a good memory, and is particularly astute when dealing with business and financial matters. He tends to be quietly spoken and a little reserved, but he does have sufficient strength of character to make his views known and attain his ambitions. He is very loyal to his family and friends.

## Wood Snake: 1905, 1965
The Wood Snake has a friendly temperament and a good understanding of human nature. He is able to communicate well with others and often has many friends and admirers. He is witty, intelligent and ambitious. He has numerous interests and prefers to live in a quiet, stable environment where he can work without too much interference. He enjoys the arts and usually derives much pleasure from collecting paintings and antiques. His advice—particularly on social and domestic matters—is often very highly valued.

## Fire Snake: 1917, 1977
The Fire Snake tends to be more forceful, outgoing and energetic than some of the other types of Snake. He is ambitious, confident, and never slow in voicing his opinions—and he can be very abrasive to those he does not like. He does, however, have many leadership qualities and can win the respect and support of many with his firm and resolute manner. He usually has a good sense of humour, a wide circle of friends, and a very active social life. The Fire Snake is also a keen traveller.

**Earth Snake: 1929, 1989**
The Earth Snake is charming, amusing, and has a very amiable manner. He is conscientious and reliable in his work and approaches everything he does in a level-headed and sensible way. He can, however, tend to err on the cautious side and never likes to be hassled into making a decision. He is extremely adept in dealing with financial matters and is a shrewd investor. He has many friends and is very supportive towards the members of his family.

# Prospects for the Snake in 1992

The Chinese New Year starts on 4 February 1992. Until then the old year, the year of the Goat, is still making its presence felt.

The year of the Goat (15 February 1991–3 February 1992) will have been a favourable year for the Snake. He will have been able to set about his various activities and interests in his own determined and inimitable way and will have made considerable progress. Just as importantly, he will have impressed many around him—including some who wield great influence—and this could prove important to him over the next few years.

However, the Snake may have had to contend with a few problems during the Goat year. While not serious, these could have caused him some worry and concern. In dealing with these problems the Snake should remember that, despite his sometimes rather solitary and independent nature, he cannot tackle everything on his own. He will find that his family, friends and colleagues are happy to help and assist him. This is something he would do well to bear in mind not only as the Goat year ends but in the year ahead as well. Many Snakes may also have had to help someone close to them over the year, and their support and caring attitude will have done much to help.

Towards the end of the Goat year the Snake could enjoy some good news concerning his work or financial matters.

He should also accept any invitations to social functions that he receives, even if he must alter his plans in order to do so. These functions are likely to prove most enjoyable and could help to widen his circle of friends and acquaintances even further.

The year of the Monkey starts on 4 February 1992 and it will be a mixed year for the Snake. In some aspects of his life he can look forward to doing well and making much progress, but in others the Snake could have to contend with delays and a few awkward problems.

To look at the more positive aspects first, the Snake is likely to do well in financial matters, and any Snake who may have been experiencing financial problems will find his situation considerably eased over the year. If the Snake is able to make any investments in 1992, these are likely to work out well for him and could prove a valuable asset in the future. However, despite the generally advantageous trends in financial matters, the Snake should still be wary of any 'get-rich-quick' schemes that he hears about, and of being misguided by extravagant claims or false promises. Provided he is prudent and careful and follows his own judgement, the Snake will do well in financial matters.

The Snake can also look forward to enjoying considerable success with his hobbies and interests, particularly if they allow him to use his creative or intellectual skills in any way. In addition, many Snakes will be able to turn one of their interests or skills to profitable use over the year, and this will give them a tremendous amount of satisfaction and pleasure.

Any Snake involved in education is also likely to be pleased with his progress, and for those eager to add to their skills or obtain another qualification, this would be an excellent year to do so. Likewise those Snakes seeking employment should consider taking advantage of any training scheme or course they may be eligible for, as this would do much to enhance their future prospects.

The Snake will have some highly enjoyable times with

his family and friends over the year. His domestic life is likely to be content and settled, and those around him will be pleased to help and assist him in his various activities. The Snake should not hesitate to seek their advice should there be any matter causing him concern.

Life for the single Snake will be particularly enjoyable in 1992, with plenty of opportunities to meet others. Many single Snakes could meet their future partner over the year or get engaged or married. Romance is very well aspected in 1992, with the summer and latter part of the year being especially happy times.

There are, however, certain areas that could prove troublesome for the Snake in 1992. Although he will make progress in his work over the year, he could find that it takes him longer to get things accomplished than he would like. While he should still pursue any opportunity and set about his work in his usual conscientious manner, his gains over the year are likely to be more in the form of increased experience and knowledge than rapid progress. To compensate for this, the knowledge and skills that he does obtain over the year will help to lay the foundation for the excellent progress he will make in 1993—the year of the Rooster, one of the most favourable of all years for the Snake.

The Snake could also be faced with some annoying problems in 1992. These could concern the delay of items he has ordered, or they could be problems of a bureaucratic nature. The Snake should therefore pay very careful attention to any important correspondence or official forms that he receivés over the year; a mistake or oversight could involve him in a lot of additional correspondence and worry. In all matters of paperwork, the Snake needs to be most careful.

Another area in which the Snake could experience problems concerns any long-distance travelling that he proposes to undertake, as he could find that his travel plans do not run as smoothly as he had hoped. All Snakes would be advised to check their itineraries and travel arrangements very carefully before setting out on any lengthy journey. Failure to do so could result in delays and a disappointing journey. Shorter trips and local travelling should be problem free, and the breaks and short holidays that the Snake does take over the year should be most pleasurable.

Generally, provided the Snake sets about his various activities in his usual cautious manner, he will not fare too badly over the year. He will do well in financial matters, and his happy domestic and social life will compensate greatly for any disappointments or problems that he has to overcome. Admittedly his progress may not be as great or as swift as he would have liked, but the experience that he gains will help prepare him for the considerable success he can look forward to in 1993.

As far as the different types of Snake are concerned, 1992 will be a quiet year for the **Metal Snake**. His family and social life will be most pleasurable, with several memorable functions to attend and some family celebrations likely. The Metal Snake will also be fortunate in financial matters over the year, and should he find himself in a position to make an investment or some prudent alterations to his financial situation he will find these will work out well for him. In work matters the Metal Snake must resist being either impatient or relying too much on his own resources. He should also be wary of committing himself to too many activities at any one time, as he could find that it takes him longer to get things done than he anticipated. If he feels he is under too much pressure he should not hesitate to ask for assistance; he will find others generally pleased to help and co-operate with him. His prospects, particularly as far as his work is concerned, will show a dramatic improvement in the latter part of the year—an improvement that will carry on into 1993.

This will be an interesting year for the **Water Snake**,

partly because he will encounter several tempting opportunities or be given new and increased responsibilities that
will greatly enhance his future prospects. He is also likely
to enjoy an improvement in his financial situation over the
year. However, despite these seemingly good trends the
Water Snake will need to exercise a certain amount 'of
restraint and self-discipline. His ambitions must be curbed
somewhat, and however noble his intentions he must not
take on more commitments than he can sensibly handle,
and he should not take any irrevocable decision without
giving the matter considerable thought. For the Water
Snake, 1992 should be a year of steady progress and
planning, with his major gains coming through in 1993,
the year of the Rooster. The Water Snake is likely to have
some happy times with his family and friends over the
year, and be delighted with the progress and achievements
of a young member of his family. Although he will have
many demands on his spare time, it is essential that he does
set aside a regular time for recreational pursuits and for
doing something unrelated to his usual activities—he will
feel considerably better for doing so. Also, if he does not
take much exercise during the day, he will notice a general
improvement in his well-being if he takes up some suitable
sporting activity or exercise course. Swimming, jogging or
walking could all be ideal and favourable activities for him
to consider.

This will be a generally enjoyable year for the **Wood
Snake**, and he can look forward to making a reasonable
amount of progress with many of his activities. He will lead
a most pleasant domestic and social life and will be much
in demand with his family and friends. Many Wood Snakes
will see an addition to their family over the year or achieve
a personal goal that will give rise to much celebration.
They will also be able to devote time over the year to their
various hobbies and interests—these will not only give
satisfaction but could develop in a very constructive and
unexpected manner, leading to new friendships or another

source of income. If the Wood Snake is interested in art, music, writing or some other creative pursuit, he should not hesitate to promote his work and talents as they are likely to be favourably received. The Wood Snake may, however, find that he does have to overcome some problems over the year—particularly of a bureaucratic nature—and this could cause him to alter or delay some of his longer-term plans. As for all Snakes, in 1992 the Wood Snake will need to be especially careful when dealing with important forms and paperwork.

This will be a reasonable year for the **Fire Snake**. He will find that others are prepared to support and co-operate with him in his various activities, and he should not hesitate to seek the opinions of others should he be faced with any problems or important decisions over the year— he will be grateful for the advice and reassurance he is given. The Fire Snake will be generally fortunate in financial matters over the year, although he should keep a close watch over his spending as he could find that his general level of expenditure is greater than he thought—a few prudent alterations will do much to improve his financial situation. Any Fire Snake who may have felt lonely in recent years would do well to join a local society or get in contact with others who share similar interests. The year is very well aspected for making new friends and for leading a pleasant and active social life, and 1992 will be a year many Fire Snakes will enjoy.

This will be a mixed year for the **Earth Snake**. Throughout the year he will need to set about his various activities with considerable care, and should avoid taking risks or ignoring the advice of others. If he is not careful he could find himself involved in some awkward situations which, although not necessarily his fault, could take some while to sort out. This is not a year when he can afford to act independently or take risks. However, despite this and any problems or obstacles that he has to overcome in the year, 1992 need not be a bad year for him. He can look forward to having some truly splendid times with his family and friends, and will lead a pleasant and enjoyable social life. He will also be fortunate in financial matters and successful in purchasing things for himself and his home at some most favourable prices. Indeed, by remaining alert he will find several remarkable bargains over the year. The Earth Snake is also likely to derive a lot of pleasure from outdoor activities and could find gardening, walking, following sport or some other out-of-door pursuit particularly pleasurable. He will also obtain a great deal of satisfaction from a new hobby or interest that he takes up, and if there has been a subject that has been intriguing him, this would be an excellent year to find out more about it.

**Action Plan for the Snake in 1992**
This will be a good year for you providing you plan your activities with care and go after specific objectives. Your progress will not be so good, however, if you try to tackle too many things at any one time or drive yourself too hard. Be sensible in your activities, plan and aim only for particular goals. As a Snake, with your very wide interests, it is all too easy for you to get distracted, and this is something you need to guard against in 1992.

Avoid the temptation to gamble or get involved in any high-risk enterprise. With care and prudence you can do very well in financial matters and your financial situation could show a considerable improvement over the year.

As a Snake you also have a tendency to keep your feelings and worries to yourself. In 1992 do try to be more open with others—you will find this to be both helpful and reassuring. Also try to get out and about a little more, attend more social functions, and give yourself time to relax and unwind.

If you experience any problems or have a clash of opinion with someone, do not let the situation get you down. Agree to disagree, compromise or find some amicable solution. Do not waste time worrying about any awkward situation that may have arisen—worry achieves very little and will only distract you from more profitable activities.

Give some thought to your long-term objectives and ambitions. 1993 will be a year of super progress for you, and any plans and ideas that you draw up in 1992 will be very helpful to you in the not-too-distant future.

## Famous Snakes

Muhammad Ali, Ann-Margret, Paddy Ashdown, Ronnie Barker, William Blake, Brahms, Raymond Burr, Dick Cheney, Julie Christie, Len Deighton, Fats Domino, Bob Dylan, Stefan Edberg, Elgar, Mahatma Gandhi, Greta Garbo, Art Garfunkel, J. Paul Getty, W.E. Gladstone, Graham Gooch, Princess Grace of Monaco, Linda Gray, Bob Hawke, Nigel Hawthorne, Denis Healey, Howard Hughes, Rev. Jesse Jackson, Derek Jameson, Griff Rhys Jones, Gordon Kaye, J.F. Kennedy, Msgnr Bruce Kent, Carole King, Abraham Lincoln, Dame Vera Lynn, Magnus Magnusson, Mao Tse-tung, Nigel Mansell, Dean Martin, Henri Matisse, Robert Mitchum, Nasser, Bob Newhart, Aristotle Onassis, Jacqueline Onassis, Pablo Picasso, Edgar Allan Poe, André Previn, Brian Redhead, Jean-Paul Sartre, Franz Schubert, Brooke Shields, Paul Simon, Delia Smith, John Thaw, David Waddington, Oprah Winfrey, Victoria Wood, Virginia Woolf, Mike Yarwood, Susannah York.

# The Horse

| | | |
|---|---|---|
| 25 January 1906 | to | 12 February 1907 | *Fire Horse* |
| 11 February 1918 | to | 31 January 1919 | *Earth Horse* |
| 30 January 1930 | to | 16 February 1931 | *Metal Horse* |
| 15 February 1942 | to | 4 February 1943 | *Water Horse* |
| 3 February 1954 | to | 23 January 1955 | *Wood Horse* |
| 21 January 1966 | to | 8 February 1967 | *Fire Horse* |
| 7 February 1978 | to | 27 January 1979 | *Earth Horse* |
| 27 January 1990 | to | 14 February 1991 | *Metal Horse* |

## The Personality of the Horse

Everyone has talent. What is rare is the courage to follow the talent to the dark place where it leads.

—*Erica Jong: a Horse.*

The Horse is born under the signs of elegance and ardour. He has a most engaging and charming manner and is usually very popular. He loves meeting people and likes attending parties and other large social gatherings.

He is a lively character and enjoys being the centre of attention. He has considerable leadership qualities and is much admired for his honest and straightforward manner. He is an eloquent and persuasive speaker and has a great love of discussion and debate. The Horse also has a particularly agile mind and can assimilate facts remarkably quickly.

He does, however, have a fiery temper and, although his outbursts are usually short-lived, he can often say things which he will later regret. He is also not particularly good at keeping secrets.

The Horse has many interests and involves himself in a wide variety of activities. He can, however, get involved in so much that he can often waste his energies on projects which he never has time to complete. He also has a tendency to change his interests rather frequently and will often get caught up with the latest craze or 'in thing' until something better or more exciting turns up.

The Horse also likes to have a certain amount of freedom and independence in the things that he does. He hates being bound by petty rules and regulations and as far as possible he likes to feel that he is answerable to no one but himself. But, despite this spirit of freedom, he still likes to have the support and encouragement of others in his various enterprises.

Due to his many talents and likeable nature, the Horse will often go far in life. He enjoys challenges and is a methodical and tireless worker. However, should things work against him and he fail with any of his enterprises, it will take a long time for him to recover and pick up the pieces again. Success to the Horse means everything. To fail is a disaster and a humiliation.

The Horse likes to have variety in his life and he will try his hand at many different things before he settles down to one particular job. Even then, he will probably remain alert to see if there are any new and better opportunities for him to take up. The Horse has a restless nature and can easily get bored. He does, however, excel in any position which allows him sufficient freedom to act on his own initiative or brings him into contact with a lot of people.

Although the Horse is not particularly bothered about accumulating great wealth, he handles his finances with care and will rarely experience any serious financial problems.

The Horse also enjoys travel and he loves visiting new and far-away places. At some stage during his life he will be tempted to live abroad for a short period, and due to his adaptable nature he will find that he will fit in well wherever he goes.

The Horse pays a great deal of attention to his appearance and usually likes to wear smart, colourful, and rather distinctive clothes. He is very attractive to the opposite sex and will often have many romances before he settles down. He is loyal and protective to his partner, but despite his family commitments he still likes to retain a certain measure of independence and have the freedom to carry on with his own interests and hobbies. He will find that he is especially well suited to those born under the signs of the Tiger, Goat, Rooster and Dog. The Horse can also get on well with the Rabbit, Dragon, Snake, Pig, and another Horse, but he will find the Ox too serious and intolerant for his liking. The Horse will also have difficulty getting on with the Monkey and the Rat—the Monkey is very inquisitive and the Rat seeks security—and both will resent the Horse's rather independent ways.

The female Horse is usually most attractive and has a friendly outgoing personality. She is highly intelligent, has many interests, and is alert to everything that is going on around her. She particularly enjoys outdoor pursuits and often likes to take part in sport and keep-fit activities. She also enjoys travel, literature, and the arts, and is a very good conversationalist.

Although the Horse can be stubborn and rather self-centred, he does have a considerate nature and is often willing to help others. He has a good sense of humour and will usually make a favourable impression wherever he goes. Provided he can curb his slightly restless nature and keep a tight control over his temper, the Horse will go through life making friends, taking part in a multitude of different activities, and generally achieving many of his objectives. His life will rarely be dull.

# The Five Different Types of Horse

In addition to the twelve signs of the Chinese zodiac, there are five elements, and these have a strengthening or moderating influence on the sign. The effects of the five elements on the Horse are described below, together with the years that the elements were exercising their influence. Therefore all Horses born in 1930 and 1990 are Metal Horses, those born in 1942 are Water Horses, and so on.

**Metal Horse: 1930, 1990**
This Horse is bold, confident and forthright. He is ambitious and also a great innovator. He loves challenges and takes great delight in sorting out complicated problems. He likes to have a certain amount of independence in the things that he does and resents any outside interference. The Metal Horse has charm and a certain charisma, but he can also be very stubborn and rather impulsive. He usually has many friends and enjoys an active social life.

**Water Horse: 1942**
The Water Horse has a friendly nature, a good sense of humour, and is able to talk intelligently on a wide range of topics. He is astute in business matters and is quick to take advantage of any opportunities that arise. He does, however, have a tendency to get easily distracted and can change his interests—and indeed his mind—rather frequently, and this can often work to his detriment. He is nevertheless very talented and can often go far in life. He pays a great deal of attention to his appearance and is usually smart and well turned out. He loves to travel and also enjoys sport and other outdoor activities.

## Wood Horse: 1894, 1954

The Wood Horse has a most agreeable and amiable nature. He communicates well with others and, like the Water Horse, is able to talk intelligently on many different subjects. He is a hard and conscientious worker and is held in high esteem by his friends and colleagues. His opinions and views are often sought and, given his imaginative nature, he can quite often come up with some very original and practical ideas. He is usually widely read and likes to lead a busy social life. He can also be most generous and often holds high moral viewpoints.

## Fire Horse: 1906, 1966

The element of Fire combined with the temperament of the Horse creates one of the most powerful forces in the Chinese zodiac. The Fire Horse is destined to lead an exciting and eventful life and to make his mark in his chosen profession. He has a forceful personality and his intelligence and resolute manner bring him the support and admiration of many. He loves action and excitement and his life will rarely be quiet. He can, however, be rather blunt and forthright in his views and does not take kindly to interference in his own affairs or to obeying orders. He is a flamboyant character, has a good sense of humour, and will lead a very active social life.

## Earth Horse: 1918, 1978

This Horse is considerate and caring. He is more cautious than some of the other types of Horse, but he is wise, perceptive and extremely capable. Although he can be rather indecisive at times, he has considerable business acumen and is very astute in financial matters. He has a quiet, friendly nature and is well thought of by his family and friends.

# Prospects for the Horse in 1992

The Chinese New Year starts on 4 February 1992. Until then the old year, the year of the Goat, is still making its presence felt.

The year of the Goat (15 February 1991-3 February 1992) will have been a busy year for the Horse. Many will have travelled considerable distances over the year, changed their accommodation and led a generally pleasant and busy social life. The Horse will also have made a modest amount of progress in his work over the year, although he may not have achieved as much as he would have liked.

Indeed, the main benefits of the Goat year for the Horse are likely to have been in the form of experience and increased skills rather than rapid progress. The knowledge the Horse has gained over the year will serve him well in the year of the Monkey—a highly favourable year for him.

The Horse would do well, in what remains of the Goat year, to listen to any advice he is given by those with experience, and should use any opportunity that he has to discuss his future hopes and plans with others. Likewise if he is able to draw up a set of priorities for the forthcoming year and finish off outstanding matters he will find this will be time usefully spent.

The latter part of the Goat year could, however, prove an expensive time for the Horse, and he would do well to keep an eye on his level of spending and at the same time avoid getting involved in any risky or speculative ventures. He should also deal carefully with any important items of correspondence he receives at this time, as a delayed reply or an oversight on his part could be to his detriment.

The year of the Monkey starts on 4 February 1992 and it is going to be a most favourable year for the Horse. He can look forward to making substantial progress with many of his activities and find that those around him are most willing to support and co-operate with him.

In his work he should not hesitate to pursue any opportunities that arise, and many Horses can look forward to promotion or to obtaining a new, more responsible and lucrative position. Similarly, those Horses seeking employment should go after any openings and opportunities that come their way; with the favourable trends that exist they will find their persistence and determination rewarded.

This is also a favourable time for the Horse to advance any ideas he has or to start any new projects that he may have been contemplating. However, in any new venture the Horse should make sure that he has the support of others and should resist the temptation, no matter how strong, to do things independently. Over the year the Horse will accomplish considerably more if he joins forces with others than if he tries to accomplish everything single-handed.

The Horse will lead a content and settled home life in 1992 and also a most pleasant social life. As with the year of the Goat, 1992 is a good year for any Horse who wishes to move and they are likely to find any change in residence will work out well for them, although the whole process might prove more time-consuming and costly than they anticipated. Alternatively many Horses will carry out alterations and improvements to their property; again they will be pleased with the results.

The single Horse will have plenty of opportunities to meet with others over the year, although he should be wary of entering into any commitment after only a short friendship. However, provided he is sensible in his relationships with others and lets any new friendship develop gradually and in its own time, the Horse is likely to find that friendship growing on a more secure and solid foundation.

Although the Horse will enjoy reasonably good health over the year, if he does find himself under any great pressure and feels unduly tired he should allow himself the opportunity to rest and unwind. By so doing he will accomplish more than if he continued to drive himself while feeling tired and stale. As far as possible the Horse should spread his activities out as much as he can and avoid putting himself under pressure or rushing projects just to get them completed. Time is on his side.

There will be opportunities for the Horse to travel over the year, and while he will thoroughly enjoy the journeys and holidays that he takes, it would be preferable if he took things steadily while he was away rather than rushing around visiting places at a frantic pace. By taking his time he will find his travels much more restorative and enjoyable.

The Horse will be generally fortunate in financial matters in 1992, although he does need to be careful before making any sizeable purchase or entering into any large financial commitment. He should check the terms of any agreement very carefully and make sure that he can meet any repayment costs that he might incur; he should also try to ensure that he is dealing with a reputable company. Provided he is careful he will do well in financial matters, but if he is careless or complacent, he could easily find himself involved in more expense than is necessary.

Generally 1992 will be an enjoyable year for the Horse, and he can look forward to making substantial progress in his work and in many of his other activities. He should not hesitate to pursue any opportunity or to promote any ideas that he has. This will be a very good year for him, and providing he exercises good sense and caution in his handling of financial matters, it will be a year of progress, prosperity and good fortune.

As far as the different types of Horse are concerned, 1992 will be a highly satisfying year for the **Metal Horse**. However, in order to get the best results from the year and to take advantage of the auspicious trends that exist, he should plan his various activities with care, drawing up a set of priorities for the year. If he does not, he could easily waste his energies on trying to do too much, and end up with very little to show for all his efforts. By restricting his activities and having some specific objectives to aim for, the Metal Horse will do extremely well. His family and friends will also be most supportive to him over the year. He can look forward to having some good and happy times with his family in 1992 and also to attending some prestigious social functions. At some time, however, he may be concerned about the well-being of a good friend, and while he may not want to appear to be interfering, any help, assistance or advice he can offer will be thoroughly appreciated. The Metal Horse could be lucky in financial matters over the year—particularly with the fruition of an investment or savings policy, or through a favourable business transaction. Despite this good fortune he should still be very careful before he re-invests any spare cash. The Metal Horse can look forward to taking several short breaks or holidays over the year, and these are likely to prove most enjoyable—especially if he chooses destinations he has not visited before and which appeal to his adventurous nature.

This will be an excellent year for the **Water Horse**, and his efforts, determination and hard work over the last few years will be rewarded either with promotion or new responsibilities. There will be plenty of opportunities for him to pursue, and he should set about his activities in a positive and determined manner. With his fine persuasive skills and the favourable trends that exist, his progress over the year can be quite considerable. In addition to doing well in work matters he will be much in demand with his family and friends. He will lead an active social life, and many Water Horses will also play a key role in arranging an important family gathering. The Water Horse will enjoy the travelling that he undertakes in 1992, although it would be very much in his interests to plan his itinerary and travel arrangements carefully before leaving, and to allow sufficient time for the necessary travel documents to reach him. The Water Horse will derive considerable pleasure from his hobbies and interests over the year, and if he can set aside a regular time to do something that is unrelated to his usual daytime activities he will find this will be highly valuable for him.

The year of the Monkey favours new ideas and innovation, and the **Wood Horse**, with his wide interests and keen mind, will certainly come up with plans and suggestions that will find favour with others. Indeed, in all his activities the Wood Horse should not hesitate to advance his own ideas, skills and talents as much as he can, and he should act boldly and positively. His progress over the year can be tremendous—but a lot depends on his determination and persistence. The Wood Horse will do especially well in work matters and is likely to be promoted or to move to a more satisfying and rewarding position. He can also look forward to having some very happy times with his family and friends. While there could be a domestic matter that arises over the year and gives him cause for concern, he should not hesitate to discuss his views and concerns openly or, if need be, to seek the advice of others. To do nothing could only make the matter worse and take the edge off what could be a very good year for him. Many Wood Horses will move or carry out alterations to their property over the year, and while this could put some pressure on them at the time, they will be pleased with how things work out.

The year of the Monkey will be a year of change for the **Fire Horse**, and over the year he will be able to better his position and go a long way towards realizing his considerable potential. Throughout the year he should pursue the many opportunities that come along and should bring his own skills and talents to the attention of others. There will also be opportunities to advance in his work, and the prospects are highly favourable for promotion or for widening his experience by taking a completely different type of job. Those Fire Horses seeking employment are also likely to find that their efforts and persistence will be rewarded—and probably at the moment when they least expect it. His family commitments and social life will take up much of his spare time and he is likely to lead a very happy and contented domestic life. One word of warning though: the Fire Horse needs to be careful if he is to undertake any strenuous activity over the year. There is a risk that he could strain himself and cause himself a certain amount of discomfort.

This will be an interesting and varied year for the **Earth Horse**. He will do well in most of his activities, although some of his plans may have to be revised in order to fit in with changing circumstances or to accommodate the wishes of others. Despite this and any moments of uncertainty that he may face over the year, the Earth Horse will be generally pleased with how the year develops and the way in which his various activities work out. He should, however, remain mindful of the views of his family and friends over the year, and some advice that he is given by a close relation or friend will prove most important and pertinent to his present situation. It would also be in the Earth Horse's interests to watch his level of spending as the year goes by and, if he finds his resources stretched, a few prudent alterations to the level of his outgoings will do much to ease the situation. The Earth Horse will do well in educational matters and, if there is a new hobby or subject that interests him, this would be an ideal year to find out more about it. He can also look forward to leading an enjoyable social life over the year, and the summer months are likely to be a special and memorable time for him.

### Action Plan for the Horse in 1992

This will be a splendid year for you. However, in order to get the most from the year try to have some idea of what you want to achieve; set yourself some specific goals to aim for. If you do not, there is a danger you could drift through the year without taking advantage of the highly favourable trends that exist.

Go after the opportunities that arise. With determination and a positive approach your gains over the year can be quite considerable, especially as far as your work is concerned.

Involve others in your various activities, for although as a Horse you like to retain a certain amount of independence in the things you do, your progress will be swifter and certainly greater if you enlist the support of others.

Try not to rush through any projects that you might be involved with and, as far as possible, spread your activities out over the course of the year. Avoid putting yourself under pressure by trying to do too much in a short time.

Your family and friends will be most supportive to you over the year, and if you need a second opinion or advice do not hesitate to ask for it—help and assistance will be readily forthcoming. Your social and domestic life are also likely to be most contented and enjoyable, making this a pleasing, happy and prosperous year for you.

## Famous Horses

Neil Armstrong, Rowan Atkinson, James Baker, King Baudoin of Belgium, Samuel Beckett, Leonard Bernstein, Sir John Betjeman, Karen Black, Nicholas Brady, Leonid Brezhnev, Ray Charles, Chopin, Sean Connery, Billy Connolly, Catherine Cookson, Ronnie Corbett, Elvis Costello, Jim Davidson, Anne Diamond, Clint Eastwood, Thomas Alva Edison, Linda Evans, Chris Evert, Harrison Ford, Aretha Franklin, Bob Geldof, Billy Graham, Larry Grayson, Rolf Harris, Ted Hughes, Douglas Hurd, Gerald

Kaufman, Nikita Khrushchev, Robert Kilroy-Silk, Neil Kinnock, Dr Helmut Kohl, Norman Lamont, Eddie Large, Lenin, Annie Lennox, Syd Little, Paul McCartney, Harold Macmillan, Nelson Mandela, Princess Margaret, Spike Milligan, Sir Isaac Newton, Harold Pinter, J.B. Priestley, Louis Pasteur, Puccini, Rembrandt, Ruth Rendell, Franklin D. Roosevelt, Anwar Sadat, Peter Sissons, Lord Snowdon, Alexander Solzhenitsyn, Barbra Streisand, John Travolta, Freddie Trueman, Mike Tyson, Vivaldi, Lord Whitelaw, Andy Williams, the Duke of Windsor, Steve Wright, Tammy Wynette, Boris Yeltsin, Michael York.

# The Goat

| | | | |
|---|---|---|---|
| 13 February 1907 | to | 1 February 1908 | *Fire Goat* |
| 1 February 1919 | to | 19 February 1920 | *Earth Goat* |
| 17 February 1931 | to | 5 February 1932 | *Metal Goat* |
| 5 February 1943 | to | 24 January 1944 | *Water Goat* |
| 24 January 1955 | to | 11 February 1956 | *Wood Goat* |
| 9 February 1967 | to | 29 January 1968 | *Fire Goat* |
| 28 January 1979 | to | 15 February 1980 | *Earth Goat* |
| 15 February 1991 | to | 3 February 1992 | *Metal Goat* |

## The Personality of the Goat

Don't part with your illusions. When they are gone, you may still exist, but you have ceased to live.

*—Mark Twain: a Goat.*

The Goat is born under the sign of art. He is imaginative, creative and has a good appreciation of the finer things in life.

He has an easy-going nature and prefers to live in a relaxed and pressure-free environment. He hates any sort of discord or unpleasantness and does not like to be bound by a strict routine or rigid timetable. The Goat is not one to be hurried against his will but, despite his seemingly relaxed approach to life, he is something of a perfectionist and when he starts work on a project he is certain to give of his best.

The Goat usually prefers to work in a team rather than on his own. He likes to have the support and encouragement of others, and if left to deal with matters on his own he can get very worried and tends to view things rather pessimistically. Wherever possible the Goat will leave major decision-making to others while he concentrates on his own pursuits. If, however, he feels particularly strongly about a certain matter or has to defend his position in any way, he will act with great fortitude and precision.

The Goat has a very persuasive nature and often uses his considerable charm to get his own way. He can, however, be rather hesitant about letting his true feelings be known and if he were prepared to be more forthright he would do much better as a result.

The Goat tends to have a quiet, somewhat reserved nature but when he is in company that he likes he can often become the centre of attention. He can be highly amusing, a marvellous host at parties, and a superb entertainer. Whenever the spotlight falls on the Goat, his adrenalin starts to flow and he can be assured of giving a sparkling performance—particularly if it allows him to use his creative skills in any way.

Of all the signs in the Chinese zodiac, the Goat is probably the most gifted artistically. Whether it is in the theatre, literature, music or art, the Goat is certain to make a lasting impression. He is a born creator and is rarely happier than when occupied in some artistic pursuit. But even in this the Goat does well to work with others rather than on his own. He needs inspiration and a guiding influence, and when he has found his true *métier* he can often receive widespread acclaim and recognition.

In addition to his liking for the arts, the Goat is usually quite religious and often has a deep interest in nature, animals and the countryside. The Goat is also fairly athletic and there are many who have excelled in some form of sporting activity.

Although the Goat is not particularly materialistic or concerned about finance, he will find that he will usually be lucky in financial matters and will rarely be short of the necessary funds to tide himself over. He is, however, rather indulgent and tends to spend his money as soon as he receives it rather than make provision for the future.

The Goat usually leaves home when he is young but he will always maintain strong links with his parents and the other members of his family. He is also rather nostalgic and is well known for keeping mementos of his childhood and souvenirs of places that he has visited. His home will not be particularly tidy but he knows where everything is and it will also be scrupulously clean.

Affairs of the heart are particularly important to the Goat and he will often have many romances before he finally settles down. Although the Goat is fairly adaptable, he prefers to live in a secure and stable environment and he will find that he is best suited to those born under the signs of the Tiger, Horse, Monkey, Pig, and Rabbit. He can also establish a good relationship with the Dragon, Snake, Rooster and another Goat, but he may find the Ox and Dog a little too serious for his liking. Neither will he care particularly for the Rat's rather thrifty ways.

The lady Goat devotes all her time and energy to the needs of her family. She has excellent taste in home furnishings and often uses her considerable artistic skills to make clothes for herself and her children. She takes great care over her appearance and can be most attractive to the opposite sex. Although she is not the most well-organized of people, her engaging manner and delightful sense of humour create a favourable impression wherever she goes. She is also a good cook and usually gets much pleasure from gardening and outdoor pursuits.

The Goat can win friends easily and people generally feel relaxed in his company. He has a kind and understanding nature and although he can occasionally be stubborn he can, with the right support and encouragement, live a happy and very satisfying life. And the more he can use his creative skills, the happier he will be.

# The Five Different Types of Goat

In addition to the twelve signs of the Chinese zodiac, there are five elements, and these have a strengthening or moderating influence on the sign. The effects of the five elements on the Goat are described below, together with the years that the elements were exercising their influence. Therefore all Goats born in 1931 and 1991 are Metal Goats, those born in 1943 are Water Goats, and so on.

**Metal Goat: 1931, 1991**
This Goat is thorough and conscientious in all that he does and is capable of doing very well in his chosen profession. Despite his confident manner, he can be a great worrier and he would find it a help if he were more prepared to discuss his worries with others rather than keep them to himself. He is loyal to his family and employers and will have a small group of extremely good friends. He has good artistic taste and is usually highly skilled in some aspect of the arts. He is often a collector of antiques and his home will be very tastefully furnished.

**Water Goat: 1943**
The Water Goat is very popular and makes friends with remarkable ease. He is good at spotting opportunities but does not always have the necessary confidence to follow them through. He likes to have security both in his home life and at work and does not take kindly to change. He is articulate, has a good sense of humour, and is usually very good with children.

**Wood Goat: 1895, 1955**
This Goat is generous, kind-hearted and always eager to please. He usually has a large circle of friends and involves

himself in a wide variety of different activities. He has a very trusting nature but he can sometimes give in to the demands of others a little too easily, and it would be in his own interests if he were to stand his ground a little more often. He is usually lucky in financial matters and, like the Water Goat, is very good with children.

### Fire Goat: 1907, 1967

This Goat usually knows what he wants in life and he often uses his considerable charm and persuasive personality in order to achieve his aims. He can sometimes let his imagination run away with him and has a tendency to ignore matters which are not to his liking. He is rather extravagant in his spending and would do well to exercise a little more care when dealing with financial matters. He has a lively personality, has many friends, and loves attending parties and social occasions.

### Earth Goat: 1919, 1979

The Earth Goat has a very considerate and caring nature. He is particularly loyal to his family and friends and invariably creates a favourable impression wherever he goes. He is reliable and conscientious in his work but he finds it difficult to save and never likes to deprive himself of any little luxury which he might fancy. He has numerous interests and is often very well read. He usually gets much pleasure from following the activities of various members of his family.

# Prospects for the Goat in 1992

The Chinese New Year starts on 4 February 1992. Until then the old year, the year of the Goat, is still making its presence felt.

The year of the Goat (15 February 1991–3 February 1992) will have been a reasonably good year for the Goat.

Over the year he is likely to have led a most pleasant and enjoyable social life, and even in the closing stages of the Goat's own year there will be opportunities to meet with others and invitations to a variety of social events. Some new friends and acquaintances that the Goat will have made during the year are likely to be long lasting and of special importance to him in the future. Socially, the year of the Goat is likely to have been a splendid year for him. His family and domestic life are likely to have been happy and many Goats will have been involved with or taken part in a memorable family celebration over the course of the year.

As far as his other activities are concerned, the Goat will have enjoyed mixed fortunes. Although there will have been opportunities for progress, much will have depended upon the Goat's own persistence and determination. If the Goat has been prepared to seek out and act on the opportunities that have come his way, he will have made pleasing progress. If, however, he has been reticent or reserved in his actions, especially in following up any opportunities connected with his work, his progress will have been more modest. In the year of the Goat, the Goat does need to be positive and bold in his actions—if he bears this in mind, not only for what remains of the year of the Goat but also for the future, his progress and results will be all the more considerable, and certainly more satisfying.

The year of the Monkey starts on 4 February 1992 and it is going to be a busy and interesting year for the Goat. Admittedly not all his activities will go according to plan, and he could meet with opposition to some of his activities, but he can still look forward to making substantial progress over the year.

In his work he will continue to impress those around him, and many Goats will be promoted or be able to move to a more satisfying and rewarding position. However, the Goat needs to handle any dealings with his colleagues carefully. He cannot automatically assume that he has their support for his ideas, nor must he be reticent in letting others know of his views and feelings. Sometimes the Goat can be guilty of withdrawing into himself and concealing his true feelings; this is something he would do well to avoid in 1992.

Those Goats who are artistically inclined, and particularly those who are able to use their creative and imaginative skills in their work, are likely to do exceptionally well.

The Goat will be relatively fortunate in financial matters in 1992, and any financial difficulties he might have been experiencing will be eased over the year. However, it would be in the interests of all Goats to keep a watch on their level of expenditure. If they are not careful they could find this is greater than they thought. Those Goats tempted to use credit for their purchases should ensure that they can meet the repayment costs. Stretching their resources too far could easily lead to problems.

The Goat will also need to be careful in his handling of personal relationships over the year. He should pay attention to the views and feelings of those around him and make sure that he allows sufficient time to devote to his loved ones and their interests. As far as possible he should let others be involved in his activities, and should any disagreements or ill feeling arise he should do all in his power to bring the matter to a speedy and amicable solution. Family matters and personal relationships need careful handling, and if the Goat realizes this—and he is, after all, most adroit when handling personal relationships—all will be well. But if he ignores the feelings of others or becomes too preoccupied with his own concerns there is a danger that personal relationships will suffer. It is a warning all Goats would do well to heed.

This care in the handling of personal relationships also applies to the single Goat, particularly in the early stages of the year. The single Goat must remain especially considerate and attentive to the views and feelings of those around him, and he should also be prepared to speak frankly on anything giving him cause for concern. Although not all matters of the heart may go as smoothly as he would like, the omens are still very favourable for meeting others, for romance and for marriage. Provided the single Goat is sensible in his relationships with others, the year of the Monkey will be a most happy and memorable year for him.

The Goat will also obtain much satisfaction from outdoor activities over the year, such as gardening, walking or pursuing some sporting activity. Also, in view of this being such a favourable year for creative activities, any Goat who is artistically inclined and who is able to combine an interest such as painting or photography with being outdoors will have a particularly splendid and enjoyable time. Similarly, any Goat who is interested in taking up such pursuits will find that enrolling on a course or reading up about a particular subject will give him another interest, one which he could find both absorbing and relaxing.

The Goat will generally enjoy good health over the year, although any goat who does not get much exercise during the day will find that a regular brisk walk, a swim, or other suitable activity will do a lot to improve his well-being. Also, any Goat who tends to rush his meals or relies a lot on fast food could suffer from digestive problems, and all Goats would do well to ensure that they eat a sensible, healthy and balanced diet.

Generally the Goat will enjoy the year of the Monkey and will be content with his achievements. Provided he handles his relationships with others considerately and sets about his activities in a positive and determined manner, he will make pleasing progress over the year and do well in most of his activities.

As far as the different types of Goat are concerned, 1992 will be a relatively pleasant year for the **Metal Goat**. He will have some enjoyable times with his family and friends and will also thoroughly enjoy any holiday or short breaks that he takes over the year. Many Metal Goats will find that they have some spare time in 1992, and if this occurs they would do well to take up another interest or, if possible, to consider taking a part-time job. They will find this will be especially satisfying and an excellent use of time that they might not otherwise have usefully filled. Many Metal Goats will also carry out improvements on their property or will move during the year, and while this will work out most satisfactorily, they should pay particular attention to the paperwork involved before entering into any transaction. This applies not only to moving or to work connected with their property but also to official forms or important items of correspondence. An oversight or misinterpretation of some of the terms could cause numerous problems—problems which, with care, could have been avoided.

This will be a year of opportunity for the **Water Goat**, and he can look forward to making considerable progress with many of his activities. He will do especially well in his work, although he does need to be more assertive and to pursue any opportunities with a resolute and solid determination. With the right attitude he can make great strides in his work and reap the rewards of efforts made over recent years. His family will be supportive and encouraging, and the Water Goat would do well to discuss his plans and hopes for the future with those around him. The help and advice he is given will prove of paramount importance, and added to this he will benefit from the affection and regard shown by others for him. The Water Goat will lead a pleasant social life over the year, and many will enjoy a family celebration in the year—either a wedding in the family or the birth of a grandchild. He will be fortunate in financial matters, especially in the purchase of some furnishings, antiques or special items for his home at very advantageous prices. However, despite this success he will need to watch his level of expenditure carefully, and he would also do well to check the terms of any investment or savings policy he is considering quite thoroughly and try to ensure that he is dealing with a reputable company. Provided he is careful he will do well, but without this care things could easily go against him.

This will be an enjoyable year for the **Wood Goat**. He will make pleasing progress in his work and could be given promotion or increased responsibilities in recognition of his past efforts. He should also pursue any opportunities that arise and not be reticent about expressing his views on any matters that are causing him concern. As long as he is prepared to be bold, assertive and at the same time considerate of the views of others, his progress over the year can be considerable. His family and friends will give him much pleasure in 1992 and will support and encourage him in his various activities. However, he could be concerned about the interests of someone close to him over the year, and should not hesitate to offer any advice or help that he thinks necessary. The Wood Goat will thoroughly enjoy his main holiday of the year and it would be very much in his interests to choose his destination with care—it could prove to be one of the best holidays he has had for a long time! As has been mentioned, 1992 is a very good year for Goats with artistic skills, and any Wood Goat whose work or interests are of a creative nature should promote his work and talents as much as he can. His efforts will be most favourably received.

This will be a challenging year for the **Fire Goat** and, while some of the events that happen may not be entirely to his liking, he will emerge from the year a wiser, more confident and capable person, and this can only be to his future good. Added to this, the experience that he will gain and the work he does now will help lay the foundation for the successes he will enjoy over the next few years. In 1992 the Fire Goat will need to set about his activities in a determined but sensible way. Although he knows what he wants to achieve, there is a danger that he is trying to accomplish too much too soon and is being over-ambitious in his objectives. Provided he is resolute in his aims—and is prepared to listen to the advice of others—he will do well. The Fire Goat will have several strokes of luck as far as financial matters are concerned, and could also be fortunate in a transaction concerned with property. The Fire Goat will also have cause for a family celebration over the year—possibly by getting engaged, married or through an addition to his family.

This will be a good and generally happy year for the **Earth Goat**. He will do well in his various activities, although throughout the year he does need to consider carefully the views and feelings of those around him. As with all Goats, in 1992 his relations with others will need careful handling, and he would do well to remember that any advice or suggestions his family offer are given with his best interests at heart. To ignore the advice or to act in opposition to the wishes of others could bring discord and unhappiness. Throughout 1992 the Earth Goat should show himself to be flexible, conciliatory and willing to listen to others. He will lead a pleasant social life and will make some new and extremely good friends. He will also derive much pleasure from his various hobbies and interests, particularly any that enable him to use his considerable creative or imaginative talents. The year also favours academic pursuits, and those Earth Goats involved in education are likely to do especially well. With a determined and confident approach their progress and results could easily exceed their expectations. The summer months and later stages of the year are likely to be a most fortunate time for the Earth Goat.

**Action Plan for the Goat in 1992**
Remain positive and determined throughout the year. Go after the opportunities that occur and try to overcome any reluctance you may feel about introducing change in your life. You can achieve much over the year, but your degree of success is very much up to your own efforts, and particularly your attitude.

Handle your relationships with others with great care. Deal with any awkward situations as they occur, and make sure that others know how you feel about important issues. If you keep your feelings and thoughts to yourself you could easily be misunderstood. Resolve to be frank, open, and honest with others and you will not go far wrong.

Try to spread your activities out over the course of the year, but at the same time have some objectives to aim for. If you have any artistic talents—which indeed many Goats have—promote your work and yourself as much as you can. This is a year that favours creativity and originality, and as a Goat you are well placed to succeed and to attract some very favourable attention. If you have any creative ambitions, 1992 will be a superb year for you.

Although the year will be busy it will also be enjoyable, and your social life is likely to be most pleasant. If you are seeking new friends, do try to go out more—the Monkey, who holds the Goat in so much esteem, will certainly do his best to ensure that you will have some fun and good times in his year, and that you will be able to remember 1992 with much fondness and satisfaction.

## Famous Goats

Dame Peggy Ashcroft, Isaac Asimov, Jane Austen, Boris Becker, Ian Botham, John le Carré, Nat 'King' Cole, Catherine Deneuve, John Denver, Arthur Conan Doyle, Douglas Fairbanks, Dame Margot Fonteyn, Anna Ford, Paul Gascoigne, Paul Michael Glaser, Mikhail Gorbachev, Larry Hagman, George Harrison, Sir Edmund Hillary, Mick Jagger, Ben Kingsley, David Kossoff, Peter Lilley, Franz Liszt, Doris Lessing, Michelangelo, Cliff Michelmore, Joni Mitchell, Edwin Moses, Rupert Murdoch, Frank Muir,

Mussolini, Leonard Nimoy, Robert de Niro, Des O'Connor, Lord Olivier, Michael Palin, Cecil Parkinson, Javier Perez de Cuellar, Alain Prost, Keith Richards, Sir Malcolm Sargent, Mike Smith, Freddie Starr, Norman Tebbit, Leslie Thomas, Mark Twain, Rudolph Valentino, Vangelis, Lech Walesa, Barbara Walters, Andy Warhol, John Wayne, Bruce Willis.

# The Monkey

| | | |
|---|---|---|
| 2 February 1908 to | 21 January 1909 | *Earth Monkey* |
| 20 February 1920 to | 7 February 1921 | *Metal Monkey* |
| 6 February 1932 to | 25 January 1933 | *Water Monkey* |
| 25 January 1944 to | 12 February 1945 | *Wood Monkey* |
| 12 February 1956 to | 30 January 1957 | *Fire Monkey* |
| 30 January 1968 to | 16 February 1969 | *Earth Monkey* |
| 16 February 1980 to | 4 February 1981 | *Metal Monkey* |
| 4 February 1992 to | 22 January 1993 | *Water Monkey* |

## The Personality of the Monkey

Anything you're good at contributes to happiness.
—*Bertrand Russell: a Monkey.*

The Monkey is born under the sign of fantasy. He is imaginative, inquisitive, and loves to keep an eye on everything that is going on around him. He is never backward in offering advice or trying to sort out the problems of others. He likes to be helpful and his advice is invariably sensible and reliable.

He is intelligent, well read, and always eager to learn. He has an extremely good memory and there are many Monkeys who have made particularly good linguists. The Monkey is also a convincing talker and enjoys taking part in discussions and debates. His friendly, self-assured manner can be very persuasive and he usually has little trouble in winning people round to his way of thinking—it is for this reason that the Monkey often excels in politics and public speaking. He is also particularly adept in PR work, teaching, and any job which involves selling.

He can, however, be crafty, cunning, and occasionally dishonest, and he will seize on any opportunity to make some quick gain or outsmart his opponents. He has so much charm and guile that people often don't realize what he is up to until it is too late. But despite his resourceful nature he does run the risk of outsmarting even himself. He has so much confidence in his abilities that he rarely listens to advice or is prepared to accept help from anyone. The Monkey likes to help others but prefers to rely on his own judgement when dealing with his own affairs.

Another characteristic of the Monkey is that he is extremely good at solving problems and has a happy knack of extricating himself (and others) from the most hopeless of positions. He is the master of self-preservation.

With so many diverse talents the Monkey is able to make considerable sums of money, but he does like to enjoy life and will think nothing of spending his money on some exotic holiday or luxury which he has had his eye on. He can, however, become very envious if someone else has got what he wants.

The Monkey is an original thinker and, despite his love of company, he cherishes his independence. He has to have the freedom to act as he wants and any Monkey who feels hemmed in or bound by too many restrictions can soon become unhappy. Likewise, if anything becomes too boring or monotonous he soon loses interest and turns his attention to something else. The Monkey lacks persistence and this can often hamper his progress. He is also easily distracted, a tendency which all Monkeys should try to overcome: he should concentrate on one thing at a time, and by doing so will almost certainly achieve more in the long run.

The Monkey is a good organizer and, even though he may behave slightly erratically at times, he will invariably have some plan at the back of his mind. On the odd occasion when his plans do not quite work out, he is usually quite happy to shrug his shoulders and put it down to experience. He will rarely make the same mistake twice and throughout his life he will try his hand at many things.

The Monkey likes to impress and is rarely without followers or admirers. There are many who are attracted to him by his good looks, his sense of humour, or simply because he instils so much confidence.

Monkeys usually marry young, and to be a success their partners must allow them time to pursue their many interests and the opportunity to indulge in their love of travel. The Monkey has to have variety in his life and is especially well-suited to those born under the sociable and outgoing signs of the Rat, Dragon, Pig, and Goat. The Ox, Rabbit, Snake, and Dog will also be enchanted by the Monkey's resourceful and outgoing nature, but the Monkey is likely to exasperate the Rooster and the Horse, and the Tiger will have little patience for the Monkey's tricks. A relationship between two Monkeys will also work well—they both understand each other and are able to assist each other in their various enterprises.

The lady Monkey is intelligent, extremely observant, and a shrewd judge of character. Her opinions and views are often highly valued, and having such a persuasive nature she invariably gets her own way. The lady Monkey has many interests and involves herself in a wide variety of activities. She pays great attention to her appearance, is an elegant dresser, and likes to take particular care over her hair. She can also be a most caring and doting parent and will have many good and loyal friends.

Provided the Monkey can curb his desire to take part in all that is going on around him and concentrate on one thing at a time, he can usually achieve what he wants in life. And should he suffer any disappointments the Monkey is bound to bounce back. The Monkey is a survivor and his life is usually both colourful and very eventful.

# The Different Types of Monkey

In addition to the twelve signs of the Chinese zodiac, there are five elements, and these have a strengthening or moderating influence on the sign. The effects of the five elements on the Monkey are described below, together with the years that the elements were exercising their influence. Therefore all Monkeys born in 1920 and 1980 are Metal Monkeys, those born in 1932 and 1992 are Water Monkeys, and so on.

## Metal Monkey: 1920, 1980
The Metal Monkey is very strong-willed. He sets about everything he does with a dogged determination and often prefers to work independently rather than with others. He is ambitious, wise and confident and is certainly not afraid of hard work. He is very astute in financial matters and usually chooses his investments well. Despite his somewhat independent nature, the Metal Monkey enjoys attending parties and social occasions and is particularly warm and caring to his loved ones.

## Water Monkey: 1932, 1992
The Water Monkey is versatile, determined, and perceptive. He also has more discipline than some of the other Monkeys and is prepared to work towards a certain goal rather than be distracted by something else. He is not always open about his true intentions and when questioned can be particularly evasive. He can be sensitive to criticism but he can also be very persuasive and usually has little trouble in getting others to fall in with his plans. He has a very good understanding of human nature and relates well to others.

## Wood Monkey: 1944

This Monkey is efficient, methodical, and extremely conscientious. He is also highly imaginative and is always trying to capitalize on new ideas or learning new skills. Occasionally his enthusiasm can get the better of him and he can get very agitated when things do not quite work out as he had hoped. He does, however, have a very adventurous streak in him and is not afraid of taking risks. He also loves travel. He is usually held in great esteem by his friends and colleagues.

## Fire Monkey: 1896, 1956

The Fire Monkey is intelligent, full of vitality, and has no trouble in commanding the respect of others. He is imaginative and has wide interests, although sometimes these can distract him from more useful and profitable work. He is very competitive and always likes to be involved in everything that is going on. He can be stubborn if he does not get his own way, and he sometimes tries to indoctrinate those who are less strong-willed than himself. The Fire Monkey is a lively character, popular with the opposite sex, and extremely loyal to his partner.

## Earth Monkey: 1908, 1968

The Earth Monkey tends to be studious, well read, and can become quite distinguished in his chosen line of work. He is less outgoing than some of the other types of Monkey and prefers quieter and more solid pursuits. He has high principles, a very caring nature, and can be most generous to those less fortunate than himself. He is usually successful in handling financial matters and can become very wealthy in old age. He has a calming influence on those around him and is respected and well liked by those he meets—he is, however, especially careful about whom he lets into his confidence.

# Prospects for the Monkey in 1992

The Chinese New Year starts on 4 February 1992. Until then the old year, the year of the Goat, is still making its presence felt.

The year of the Goat (15 February 1991-3 February 1992) will have been a busy year for the Monkey. He is likely to have done well in his work and will almost certainly have sown the seeds for his advancement in the future. Indeed any efforts the Monkey makes in the closing stages of the year of the Goat towards enhancing his career prospects or bringing his talents to the attention of others will be repaid handsomely. Likewise if there are any outstanding matters that the Monkey has a chance to attend to—particularly in terms of unanswered correspondence—he will find the latter part of the year a good time to deal with them.

The Monkey is likely to have travelled considerable distances over the year of the Goat, and there will be additional opportunities for travel in the closing stages of the year. However he would do well to make sure that he sets aside some time to rest and relax. The pressures and strains of the year will have taken a lot out of him, and he will need to restore his energy for the exciting prospects that await him in his own year, the year of the Monkey.

The Christmas and New Year holidays are likely to be a most pleasant time for the Monkey, and while the holiday period could be more expensive than he anticipated, he will have some truly enjoyable times socializing and being with his family and friends.

The year of the Monkey starts on 4 February 1992 and it is going to be an excellent year for the Monkey. His hard work over recent years will be rewarded, and any ideas and plans that he has will be favourably received. His domestic and social life will also prove most enjoyable, making 1992 one of the most auspicious years that the Monkey has had for a long time.

In his work the Monkey can look forward to making considerable progress. Many Monkeys will be promoted during the year or will be given additional and more rewarding responsibilities. Those Monkeys eager to change their work will also be able to proceed with confidence, and Monkeys seeking employment will find their persistence and enterprise rewarded. Also, any Monkey who has been considering setting up his own business or becoming self-employed will be gratified by the support, help and encouragement he is given, and with the proper preparation he could do extremely well.

In addition to the favourable aspects in his work, the Monkey will also be particularly fortunate in financial matters. Many Monkeys will enjoy a considerable improvement in their finances over the year, but while there is a distinct and favourable monetary trend there are also two points that the Monkey would do well to remember: firstly, wherever possible he should avoid lending money to others; and secondly he should not get involved in any risky or dubious ventures. Provided he remains careful and vigilant in financial matters he will do extremely well, but if he takes risks he could easily end up the loser.

The Monkey will lead an active social life over the year. He will be much in demand with his friends and will be invited to a number of most pleasant social functions. Any Monkey who may have felt lonely in recent years will also notice a considerable improvement in his social life, and will have some very good opportunities to meet others— especially if he joins a local society or a club specializing in one of his interests. Those Monkeys who are unattached will have a highly pleasant year, and romance is very well aspected throughout 1992.

The Monkey's domestic life will be pleasant and settled, and his family will be most supportive of his various activities. However, the Monkey should make sure that those around him are involved in his plans and activities, and that he bears in mind their feelings and advice. To try and do too much independently (as some Monkeys might be tempted to do) will put increased pressures on him and could also prevent him from achieving as much as he would like.

The Monkey will find his travels in 1992 enjoyable, and all Monkeys would do well to make sure that they take several short breaks over the year, or at least have one main holiday. Their active life combined with the usual everyday pressures will make getting away for a proper rest essential. If a holiday is not taken the Monkey could fall victim to stress or strain and find himself tired, irritable and prone to minor ailments. By spreading his activities out and taking things at a sensible pace these problems can be avoided.

Generally this will be a truly splendid year for the Monkey. There will be plenty of opportunities for him to pursue and he will make great progress in many of his activities. In addition, his social and family life will be enjoyable and he will do well financially. This is the Monkey's own year, and with his multitude of talents, his personable nature and his ability to take advantage of opportunities that arise, 1992 will be a year in which Monkeys excel themselves.

As far as the different types of Monkey are concerned, 1992 will be a splendid year for the **Metal Monkey**. He will be able to devote considerable time and attention to his own interests, and these are likely to give much pleasure and satisfaction. It is also a favourable year for him to follow up any new interests, and if he is a collector—especially of antiques, paintings or anything old—he is likely to be fortunate in acquiring some worthy items for his collection over the course of the year. He will also enjoy some good times with his family and friends in 1992, and any Metal Monkey who may have been lonely in recent years should make every effort to get out more and meet others who share his interests: this will be a very good year for him socially. His family is likely to be most supportive over the year, and the Metal Monkey would do well to bear in mind any advice those close to him should give. Although he may not agree with all he is told he should remember that they speak with his best interests at heart, and should consider their advice carefully. The Metal Monkey will be fortunate in financial matters over the year, but he should still pay careful attention to the terms of any large financial transaction that he might be considering, especially if he decides to move house over the year. Provided he is careful and keeps a close watch on his level of expenditure he will do well, but without this care and attention he could easily be involved in more expense than is necessary.

This will be a memorable year for the **Water Monkey**. However, in order to get the best results from this most auspicious of years, he needs to give some thought to what he hopes to achieve. Without this planning, the Water Monkey could either waste his energies getting involved in too many activities or drift through the year without achieving very much. As long as he has some idea of what he wants to do, he is likely to have a splendid and most satisfying year. The Water Monkey will be much in demand with his family and friends, and could play an important role in some social functions that he attends over the year. Financial matters and travel are also favourably aspected for the Water Monkey. He will also derive much pleasure from outdoor activities, particularly from gardening, walking or by following some sporting activity. Many Water Monkeys will move or be tempted to move over the year, and while this will not entirely be problem free, the Water Monkey will be generally pleased with how the move works out for him in the long run.

This will be a superb year for the **Wood Monkey**. It will be a year in which he will be able to demonstrate his true potential and realize some of his most cherished ambitions. There will be many opportunities for him to pursue, and those Wood Monkeys wanting to change careers will be able to do so with confidence. Most Wood Monkeys who attempt a new start will move to a better, more rewarding and more lucrative position. The Wood Monkey should also try to promote his ideas as much as he can as these are likely to be received most favourably and will win the respect and support of those around him. He is also likely to be very fortunate in financial matters, although he should be wary of gambling or committing his money to highly speculative ventures. He must not let any financial success he enjoys over the year dull his usually astute manner of dealing with money. The Wood Monkey will lead a very pleasant domestic and social life in 1992, and his main holiday of the year is likely to prove one of the best he has had for a long time, leading to several new and very good friendships.

This will be an excellent year for the **Fire Monkey**, and he can look forward to making great strides in his various activities. However, in order to take advantage of these most favourable trends the Fire Monkey must be realistic in his objectives and not let his imagination run away with him. Throughout the year he should bear in mind the views and feelings of those around him and consider the advice he is given by those close to him. Although at times he might consider this advice to be a restraining influence, his family and friends do have his best interests at heart and will be a useful curb on his more risky notions. With care, good common sense and the support and advice of others, his progress over the year will be truly tremendous. Many Fire Monkeys will be promoted, move to a more rewarding position and generally do very well in their work. For any Fire Monkey who may have been experiencing problems in his work or who is seeking employment, this will be a greatly improved year for him, and his efforts and determination will be rewarded. His domestic life will also be very busy over the year, and his family will make many demands on his time. He may encounter some slight domestic problems and worries over the year, but these are unlikely to be serious or to spoil what will otherwise be a marvellous year for him.

This will be a memorable year for the **Earth Monkey**. Many will get engaged, married or have an addition to their family, and domestically and socially the entire year will be busy but also most enjoyable. Indeed, with the many demands on the Earth Monkey during the year, he should make sure that he does get some time to himself, to devote to his own interests, unwind or just catch up with any correspondence or unfinished business. The year favours academic matters, and any Earth Monkey involved in education or wishing to obtain a further qualification or new skill is likely to do very well. The knowledge and skills that he acquires in 1992 will prove invaluable in the years ahead, and any sacrifices—whether financial or personal— will be amply rewarded. Work matters are also likely to go well, with many new opportunities to pursue and prospects for rapid progress. Should there be any matter that gives the Earth Monkey cause for concern, he should not hesitate to seek the advice and opinions of those he can trust. He will certainly find much truth in the saying 'a problem shared is a problem halved.'

## Action Plan for the Monkey in 1992

This is your year; it will be enjoyable for you and one in which you can make great progress. However, in order to maximize the very good aspects that prevail during the year, you will need to bear in mind three points. Firstly, as a Monkey you tend to be very inquisitive and can get involved in too many activities at any one time. In 1992 you must try to concentrate on specific objectives and avoid getting distracted by lesser matters. Secondly, avoid risky or dubious enterprises. Thirdly, try not to rush your various activities just to get them finished. Remember, a job worth doing is a job worth doing well, and providing you remain conscientious, methodical and at your best you will greatly impress others over the year and this in turn will assist your progress.

If there is any matter giving you concern or about which you would like a second opinion, do not hesitate to seek the advice of others. Sometimes as a Monkey you tend to keep your feelings and thoughts to yourself; throughout 1992 you should try to be more open and also to involve others more in the things you do.

Domestically, socially and financially this will also be a highly favourable year for you. Enjoy it, be positive, go after your objectives and any opportunities that you see, and remember, while it is true that the aspects for the year are very good a lot depends on *you*. Make the most of your own year; with the right attitude you can make it one of the most successful you have had for a long time.

## Famous Monkeys

Cory Aquino, Michael Aspel, Bobby Ball, J.M. Barrie, David Bellamy, Jacqueline Bissett, Bjorn Borg, Frank Bough, Faith Brown, Yul Brynner, Julius Caesar, Marti Caine, Princess Caroline of Monaco, Johnny Cash, Roy Castle, Sebastian Coe, John Constable, Alistair Cooke, Mario Cuomo, Charles Dickens, Jonathan Dimbleby, Jason Donovan, Kenny Everett, Mia Farrow, Michael Fish, F. Scott Fitzgerald, Ian Fleming, Dick Francis, Paul Gauguin, Jerry Hall, Roy Hattersley, Stephen Hendry, Harry Houdini, Tony Jacklin, P.D. James, Lyndon B. Johnson, Edward Kennedy, Nigel Kennedy, Jonathan King, Cyndi Lauper, Princess Michael of Kent, Nigel Lawson, Leo McKern, Walter Matthau, Kylie Minogue, Martina Navratilova, Jack Nicklaus, Derek Nimmo, Peter O'Toole, Chris Patten, Pope John Paul II, Mario Puzo, Tim Rice, Angela Rippon, Diana Ross, Omar Shariff, Rod Stewart, Graham Taylor, Elizabeth Taylor, Dame Kiri Te Kanawa, Harry Truman, Leonardo da Vinci, John Wakeham, Brian Walden, Norman Willis, Gary Wilmot, the Duchess of Windsor, Bobby Womack.

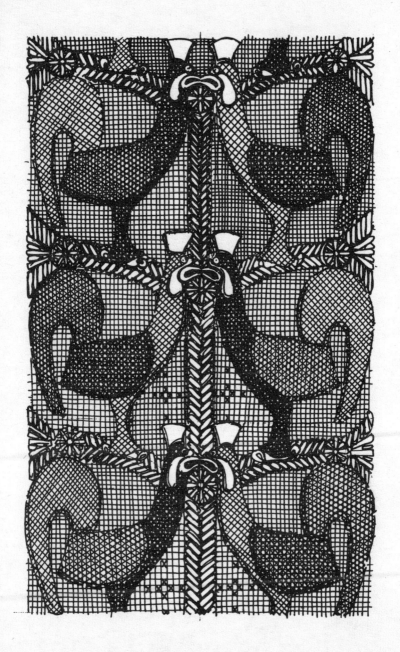

# The Rooster

| | | | |
|---|---|---|---|
| 22 January 1909 | to | 9 February 1910 | *Earth Rooster* |
| 8 February 1921 | to | 27 January 1922 | *Metal Rooster* |
| 26 January 1933 | to | 13 February 1934 | *Water Rooster* |
| 13 February 1945 | to | 1 February 1946 | *Wood Rooster* |
| 31 January 1957 | to | 17 February 1958 | *Fire Rooster* |
| 17 February 1969 | to | 5 February 1970 | *Earth Rooster* |
| 5 February 1981 | to | 24 January 1982 | *Metal Rooster* |

## The Personality of the Rooster

People must help one another; it is nature's law.
> —*Jean de La Fontaine: a Rooster.*

The Rooster is born under the sign of candour. He has a flamboyant and colourful personality and is meticulous in all that he does. He is an excellent organizer and wherever possible likes to plan his various activities well in advance.

The Rooster is highly intelligent and usually very well read. He has a good sense of humour and is an effective and persuasive speaker. He loves discussion and enjoys taking part in any sort of debate; he has no hesitation in speaking his mind and is forthright in his views. He does, however, lack tact and can easily damage his reputation or cause offence by some thoughtless remark or action. The Rooster also has a very volatile nature, and he should always try to avoid acting on the spur of the moment.

The Rooster is usually very dignified in his manner and conducts himself with an air of confidence and authority. He is adept at handling financial matters and, as with most things, he organizes his financial affairs with considerable skill. He chooses his investments well and is capable of achieving great wealth. Most Roosters save or use their money wisely, but there are a few who are the reverse and are notorious spendthrifts. Fortunately, the Rooster has great earning capacity and is rarely without sufficient funds to tide himself over.

Another characteristic of the Rooster is that he invariably carries a notebook or scraps of paper around with him. He is constantly writing himself reminders or noting down important facts lest he forgets—the Rooster cannot abide inefficiency and conducts all his various activities in an orderly, precise, and methodical manner.

The Rooster is usually very ambitious, but can be unrealistic in some of the things that he hopes to achieve. He occasionally lets his imagination run away with him and, while he does not like any interference in the things that he does, it would be in his own interests if he were to listen to the views of others a little more often. He also does not like criticism, and if he feels anybody is doubting his judgement or prying too closely into his affairs, the Rooster is certain to let his feelings be known. He can also be rather self-centred and stubborn over relatively trivial matters, but to compensate for this he is reliable, honest, and trustworthy, and this is very much appreciated by all who come into contact with him.

Roosters born between the hours of five and seven (two hours both at dawn and sundown) tend to be the most extrovert of their sign, but all Roosters like to lead an active social life and enjoy attending parties and big functions. He usually has a wide circle of friends and is able to build up influential contacts with remarkable ease. He often belongs to several clubs and societies and involves himself in a variety of different activities. He is particularly interested in the environment, humanitarian affairs, and anything affecting the welfare of others. The Rooster has a very caring nature and will do much to help those less fortunate than himself.

He also gets much pleasure from gardening and, while he may not always be able to spend as much time in the garden as he would like, his garden is invariably well-kept and extremely productive.

The Rooster is generally very distinguished in his appearance and, if his job permits, he will wear an official uniform with great pride and dignity. He is not averse to publicity and takes great delight in being the centre of attention. He often does well at PR work or any job which brings him into contact with the media. He also makes a very good teacher.

The lady Rooster leads a varied and interesting life. She involves herself in many different activities and there are some who wonder how she can achieve so much. The lady Rooster often holds very strong views and, like her male counterpart, has no hesitation in speaking her mind or telling others how she thinks things should be done. She is supremely efficient and well-organized and her home is usually very neat and tidy. The lady Rooster has a good taste in clothes and usually wears smart but very practical outfits.

The Rooster usually has a large family and as a parent takes a particularly active interest in the education of his children. He is very loyal to his partner and will find that he is especially suited to those born under the signs of the Snake, Horse, Ox, and Dragon. Provided they do not interfere too much in the Rooster's various activities the Rat, Tiger, Goat and Pig can also establish a good relationship with the Rooster, but two Roosters together are likely to squabble and irritate each other. The rather sensitive Rabbit will find the Rooster a bit too blunt for his liking, and the Rooster will quickly become exasperated by the ever-inquisitive and artful Monkey. The Rooster will also find it difficult to get on with the Dog.

If the Rooster can overcome his volatile nature and exercise more tact with some of the things that he says, he will go far in life. He is capable and talented and the Rooster will invariably make a lasting—and usually favourable—impression almost everywhere he goes.

# The Five Different Types of Rooster

In addition to the twelve signs of the Chinese zodiac, there are five elements, and these have a strengthening or moderating influence on the sign. The effects of the five elements on the Rooster are described below, together with the years that the elements were exercising their influence. Therefore all Roosters born in 1921 and 1981 are Metal Roosters, those born in 1933 are Water Roosters, and so on.

**Metal Rooster: 1921, 1981**
The Metal Rooster is a hard and conscientious worker. He knows exactly what he wants in life and sets about everything he does in a positive and determined manner. He can at times appear abrasive and he would almost certainly do better if he were sometimes more willing to reach a compromise with others rather than hold so rigidly to his firmly held beliefs. He is very articulate and most astute when dealing with financial matters. He is loyal to his friends and often devotes much energy to working for the common good.

**Water Rooster: 1933**
This Rooster has a very persuasive manner and can easily gain the co-operation of others. He is intelligent, well-read, and gets much enjoyment from taking part in discussions

and debates. He has a seemingly inexhaustible amount of energy and is prepared to work long hours in order to secure what he wants. He can, however, waste much valuable time worrying over minor and inconsequential details. He is approachable, has a good sense of humour, and is highly regarded by others.

## Wood Rooster: 1945
The Wood Rooster is honest, reliable, and often sets himself high standards. He is ambitious, but he is also more prepared to work in a team than some of the other types of Rooster. He usually succeeds in life, but he does have a tendency to get caught up in bureaucratic matters or attempt too many things all at the same time. He has wide interests, likes to travel, and is very considerate and caring to his family and friends.

## Fire Rooster: 1897, 1957
This Rooster is extremely strong-willed. He has many leadership qualities, is an excellent organizer, and is most efficient in his work. Through sheer force of character he often secures his objectives, but he does have a tendency to be very forthright and not always consider the feelings of others. If the Fire Rooster can be more tactful he can often succeed beyond his wildest dreams.

## Earth Rooster: 1909, 1969
This Rooster has a deep and penetrating mind. He is extremely efficient, very perceptive, and is particularly astute in business and financial matters. He is also persistent, and once he has set himself an objective will rarely allow himself to be deflected from achieving his aim. The Earth Rooster works hard and is held in great esteem by his friends and colleagues. He usually gets much enjoyment from the arts and takes a keen interest in the activities of the various members of his family.

# Prospects for the Rooster in 1992

The Chinese New Year starts on 4 February 1992. Until then the old year, the year of the Goat, is still making its presence felt.

The year of the Goat (15 February 1991–3 February 1992) will have been a reasonably good year for the Rooster. He is likely to have made pleasing progress in his work, and the skills, knowledge and experience he has gained over the year will serve him well in the future. Indeed, if the Rooster is keen on adding to his skills, the latter part of the Goat year is a particularly favourable time for him to do so.

The Rooster is also likely to have led a most pleasant domestic and social life in the year of the Goat, and he will have made some new and very good friends. This busy social life will continue throughout the closing stages of the year. As well as being much in demand with his family and friends, he is likely to get in touch with someone he has not seen for a very long time, and this will give him a great deal of pleasure.

Although the latter part of the year of the Goat will be an expensive time for the Rooster, he could enjoy a certain amount of luck in financial and career matters in the closing months of the year.

The year of the Monkey starts on 4 February 1992 and it is going to be a varied year for the Rooster. Some aspects of his life will go well, but in others he could experience problems. These problems are unlikely to be serious, but they could prevent him from achieving as much as he would like over the course of the year. Indeed, throughout 1992 the Rooster will need to exercise a certain amount of care with his various undertakings and avoid taking any risky or major decisions without first giving them a lot of serious thought.

To deal with the more positive aspects first, the Rooster will lead a contented and happy social life, with several very enjoyable occasions to attend over the year. With it will come the opportunity to meet with others and extend his circle of friends and acquaintances even further. The single Rooster will lead a highly pleasant social life as well, and again there will be opportunities to meet others. Romance and the affairs of the heart are especially well aspected.

The Rooster's domestic life may not, however, be as smooth as he would like. Although any problems or difficulties that arise will certainly not be serious, they will need careful handling. In case of any differences of opinion the Rooster should show himself to be conciliatory, flexible and willing to consider the viewpoints of others. With good common sense any awkward situation or difference of opinion can be easily overcome and could even result in the Rooster establishing a better understanding and rapport with those around him. Over the year the Rooster cannot afford to ignore the views and feelings of those around him. Also, if there should be someone close to him who finds him- or herself in an awkward situation or who has some difficult problem to overcome, any advice and assistance that the Rooster can offer will do much to help.

In addition to his care in handling personal relationships the Rooster will need to be careful when dealing with financial matters and should avoid taking risks or committing himself to any large financial undertaking without first examining the terms and implications closely. Provided he is careful his financial situation will steadily improve over the year, but without this care he could easily find himself with a greater expenditure than he realized. This is just not a year for the Rooster to be careless or complacent when dealing with money matters.

The Rooster also needs to be vigilant about his work. Providing he is his usual methodical self he will do well and will make a modest amount of progress, but the year of the Monkey is not one in which the Rooster can take risks or embark on major new ventures without prior thought and preparation. The Rooster needs to deal with his colleagues with care and to pay attention at all times to what is going on around him. As has already been mentioned, the previous year, the year of the Goat, was a marvellous time for him to add to his skills, and if the Rooster can continue to do this in 1992 he will find that any additional skills he is able to gain will prove of great importance to him, particularly with his prospects for his own year: 1993, the year of the Rooster. If there are any courses that interest him—whether at college, night school, by post or on the radio or television—it would certainly be in his interests to find out more, and he will find that acquiring skills and further knowledge will not only enhance his future prospects but give him much personal satisfaction as well.

The Rooster will very much enjoy any holidays that he takes in 1992, and many Roosters will travel considerable distances over the year. He will also be able to devote much time to his hobbies and interests, and will find these both relaxing and beneficial for him, especially if they provide a change from his usual daytime activites. Also, any Rooster who may have retired recently or who finds himself in the position of having lots of spare time would do well to take up a new interest in 1992 as it will prove to be a great source of pleasure not only in this year but in the future as well.

Although 1992 may not be the best of years for the Rooster, it will not be a bad year for him either. Admittedly there will be some small problems he will have to face, and he will need to be careful in his undertakings and with his dealings with others. Generally, however, most of his activities will go reasonably well and his progress during the year will serve as a useful stepping stone for the prosperity and success he will enjoy in the future and especially in 1993.

As far as the different types of Rooster are concerned,

1992 will be an interesting and challenging year for the **Metal Rooster**, although the amount of success that he enjoys over the year will very much depend upon his attitude and willingness to co-operate with others. The Metal Rooster has a very determined nature, and while he knows in his own mind what he wants, sometimes he tries to accomplish too much too soon or sets himself unrealistic targets. His resolute attitude (and occasional stubbornness) can also bring him into conflict with others, and throughout 1992 the Metal Rooster should pay careful attention to the views and advice of those around him. He should also handle his relations with others with care and diplomacy. He needs to remember that any advice he receives is often given by those who have experience and who hold his best interests dear; he should therefore consider seriously all the advice he is given. In case of any obstacles or opposition to his plans he should show himself to be flexible, understanding and, if need be, willing to compromise. If he remains obstinate he will only inflame and sour his relationships needlessly—bearing this in mind the Metal Rooster will find life considerably more pleasant and will also accomplish a great deal more. Throughout the year he will derive much pleasure from his hobbies and interests, and will lead a pleasant social life. His main holiday of the year and any short breaks that he goes on will also be most pleasurable.

This will be a pleasant year for the **Water Rooster** and, while he may find that not all the events of the year work out in his favour, he will still emerge from the year with several pleasing gains to his credit. In his work he can look forward to making a modest amount of progress, although throughout the year he will generally be kept busy and will need to remain vigilant in all his undertakings. He cannot afford to jump to hasty conclusions and must be wary of believing any rumours that he hears or of accepting information from unreliable sources. By remaining careful and his usual conscientious self he will do well and will earn the respect and support of others. Although the Water Rooster likes being involved in a good discussion or debate he should also try to avoid becoming involved in any heated argument or acrimonious exchange, as an ill-timed remark could easily backfire and cause him some difficult and unnecessary problems. The Water Rooster will, however, lead a very pleasant and active social life in 1992, and his family life will also be generally happy and settled, although to preserve domestic harmony the Water Rooster does need to involve his family in his various activities and should not hesitate to seek their opinions on any matters that are causing him concern.

This will be a busy but generally rewarding year for the **Wood Rooster**. He will do reasonably well in his work although he should avoid committing himself to more undertakings than he can sensibly handle at any one time. As far as possible it would help him if he planned his various activities in advance and if he gave some thought to his future aspirations. 1993 will be a year of fantastic progress for him, and the work that he carries out in 1992 and the plans that he makes will help to prepare him for the highly favourable trends that lie ahead. The Wood Rooster will in any case be helped by those around him, and should he need any assistance with any of his activities he will find it readily forthcoming. The Wood Rooster can also look forward to a celebration in his family—either a wedding or the birth of a grandchild. He will greatly enjoy the travelling that he undertakes over the year—especially if it is to places he has not visited before—and he will obtain much pleasure from gardening and other outdoor activities. The Wood Rooster does, however, need to be careful when lifting or moving heavy weights or handling dangerous pieces of equipment: without taking the necessary care and precautions he could easily strain or hurt himself, causing himself a certain amount of discomfort. It is better to be safe than sorry!

This will be an important year for the **Fire Rooster** and, although all the events of the year may not work out as he had hoped, there will still be several very good opportunities for him to pursue. His achievements over the year will be a prelude to the great progress he can look forward to in 1993. During the year of the Monkey, the Fire Rooster should give some serious thought to the development of his career and what he would like to achieve in the future. He should not hesitate to seek the advice and opinions of others, and he should pursue any opportunities that arise, especially if they help lead him to the realization of his aims. All the things he does—even if he meets with the occasional setback—will give him experience and prepare the way for his future prosperity. Any Fire Rooster who is seeking work or who is unhappy with what he is doing should also keep alert for opportunities to meet and talk to those who might be able to assist him. By acting positively he will be pleased with what he is able to accomplish. The Fire Rooster will also need to devote much of his time to domestic matters and the needs of his family, and he would do well to involve those around him in his various activities. This will be a very busy year for the Fire Rooster, and it is essential that he allows himself time to rest and unwind every now and again, and that he makes sure that he gets away for at least one good holiday over the year.

This will be a very significant year for the **Earth Rooster**, and while there will be some times during the year when he may feel dispirited by his apparent lack of progress, his efforts and work over the year will prove very important in the future. Not only will he gain a lot in experience and maturity over the year, but his character and sense of purpose will be strengthened by any obstacles and problems that he has to overcome. He will also win the respect and admiration of others—some of whom wield much influence—and this will help the Earth Rooster in the years to come. Throughout the year the Earth Rooster needs to set about his various activities in a positive and determined manner but at the same time take into account the views of those around him and bear in mind any advice that he is offered. By remaining careful, watchful, and his usual conscientious self he will make useful progress over the year and this will be of considerable help to him in the future. The Earth Rooster will lead a most pleasant and enjoyable social life in 1992, and he can look forward to having some splendid times with his family and friends. The Earth Rooster will find that 1992 will improve as it goes. on, and that the closing months of the year of the Monkey will be a most favourable time for him.

## Action Plan for the Rooster in 1992
1992 is very much a year when you will need to handle your relations with others with care and a good deal of tact. Although as a Rooster you like speaking your mind and are renowned for your candid and frank views, it would certainly be in your interests to think twice before passing some critical remark or entering into a contentious discussion. Try not to inflame the feelings of others unnecessarily lest you stir up trouble and problems for yourself—problems which, with care, could easily have been avoided.

Pay close attention to the views and feelings of all those around you, and try to involve your family in your various activities. Also do bear in mind any advice you are given over the year, particularly by those close to you and those with experience.

Be your usual conscientious and well-organized self in your work, and if possible take advantage of any opportunity to add to your skills and qualifications.

While in many ways you will need to be guarded in your actions in 1992 and would be wise not to take any major risks, this can still be a very important and significant year for you. Over the year give some thought to your future activities and aspirations and particularly to your career. In many ways the plans you make, the contacts you build up, and the experience you gain will place you in a marvellous position to take advantage of the highly auspicious trends that lie ahead for you, especially in 1993. 1992 is a year of preparation and planning; 1993 will be a year for putting those plans into action and for reaping the rewards of your past work.

# Famous Roosters

Kate Adie, Dame Janet Baker, Severiano Ballesteros, Michael Bentine, Dirk Bogarde, Julian Bream, Richard Briers, Michael Caine, Jasper Carrot, Enrico Caruso, Eric Clapton, Joan Collins, Leslie Crowther, Roger Daltrey, Steve Davis, Dickie Davies, Les Dawson, the Duke of Edinburgh, Gloria Estefan, Nick Faldo, Bryan Ferry, Errol Flynn, Steffi Graf, Richard Harris, Deborah Harry, Goldie Hawn, Katherine Hepburn, James Herbert, Michael Heseltine, Diane Keaton, Tom King, Bernhard Langer, D.H. Lawrence, Martyn Lewis, David Livingstone, Ken Livingstone, Somerset Maugham, Van Morrison, Paul Nicholas, Barry Norman, Yoko Ono, Donny Osmond, Dolly Parton, Roman Polanski, Nancy Reagan, Joan Rivers, Bobby Robson, Sir Harry Secombe, Carly Simon, Johann Strauss, Jayne Torvill, Sir Peter Ustinov, Richard Wagner.

# The Dog

| | | | |
|---|---|---|---|
| 10 February 1910 | to | 29 January 1911 | *Metal Dog* |
| 28 January 1922 | to | 15 February 1923 | *Water Dog* |
| 14 February 1934 | to | 3 February 1935 | *Wood Dog* |
| 2 February 1946 | to | 21 January 1947 | *Fire Dog* |
| 18 February 1958 | to | 7 February 1959 | *Earth Dog* |
| 6 February 1970 | to | 26 January 1971 | *Metal Dog* |
| 25 January 1982 | to | 12 February 1983 | *Water Dog* |

## The Personality of the Dog

To travel hopefully is a better thing than to arrive, and the true success is to labour.
—*Robert Louis Stevenson: a Dog*

The Dog is born under the signs of loyalty and anxiety. He usually holds very firm views and beliefs and is the champion of good causes. He hates any sort of injustice or unfair treatment and will do all in his power to help those less 'fortunate than himself. He has a strong sense of fair play and will be honourable and open in all his dealings.

The Dog is very direct and straightforward. He is never one to skirt round issues and speaks frankly and to the point. He can also be stubborn, but he is more than prepared to listen to the views of others and will try to be as fair as possible in coming to his decisions. He will readily give advice where it is needed and will be the first to offer assistance when things go wrong.

The Dog instils confidence wherever he goes and there are many who admire him for his integrity and resolute manner. He is a very good judge of character and he can often form an accurate impression of someone very shortly after meeting them. He is also very intuitive and can frequently sense how things are going to work out long in advance.

Despite his friendly and amiable manner, the Dog is not a big socializer. He dislikes having to attend large social functions or parties and much prefers a quiet meal with friends or a chat by the fire. The Dog is an excellent conversationalist and is often a marvellous raconteur of amusing stories and anecdotes.

He is also quick-witted and his mind is always alert. He can keep calm in a crisis and, though he does have a temper, his outbursts tend to be short-lived. The Dog is loyal and trustworthy, but if he ever feels badly let down or rejected by someone he will rarely forgive or forget.

The Dog usually has very set interests. He prefers to specialize and become an expert in a chosen area rather than dabble in a variety of different activities. He usually does well in jobs where he feels that he is being of service to others and is often suited to careers in the social services, the medical and legal professions, and also in teaching. The Dog does, however, need to feel motivated in his work. He has to have a sense of purpose in the things that he does, and if ever this is lacking the Dog can quite often drift through life without ever achieving very much. Once he has the motivation, very little can prevent him from securing his objective.

Another characteristic of the Dog is his tendency to worry and to view things rather pessimistically. Quite often these worries are totally unnecessary and are of his own making; although it may be difficult, it is a habit he should try to overcome.

The Dog is not materialistic or particularly bothered about accumulating great wealth. As long as he has the necessary money to support his family and to spend on the occasional luxury he is more than happy. However, when he does have any spare money the Dog tends to be rather a spendthrift and does not always put his money to its best use. He is also not a very good speculator and would be advised to get professional advice before entering into any long-term investment.

The Dog will rarely be short of admirers, but he is not an easy person to live with. His moods are changeable and his standards high, but he will be loyal and protective to his partner and will do all in his power to provide her with a good and comfortable home. He can get on extremely well with those born under the signs of the Horse, Pig, Tiger, and Monkey. He can also establish a sound and stable relationship with the Rat, Ox, Rabbit, Snake, and another Dog, but will find the Dragon a bit too flamboyant for his liking. He will also find it difficult to understand the creative and imaginative Goat and is likely to get highly irritated by the candid Rooster.

The female Dog is renowned for her beauty. She has a warm and caring nature, although until she knows someone well she can be both secretive and very guarded. She is highly intelligent and despite her calm and tranquil appearance she can be extremely ambitious. She enjoys sport and other outdoor activities and has a happy knack of finding bargains in the most unlikely of places. The female Dog can also get rather impatient when things do not work out as she would like.

The Dog usually has a very good way with children and can be a loving and doting parent.

The Dog will rarely be happier than when he is helping someone or doing something that will benefit others. Providing he can cure himself of his tendency to worry, he will lead a very full and active life—and in that life he will make many friends and do a tremendous amount of good.

# The Five Different Types of Dog

In addition to the twelve signs of the Chinese zodiac, there are five elements, and these have a strengthening or moderating influence on the sign. The effects of the five elements on the Dog are described below, together with the years that the elements were exercising their influence. Therefore all Dogs born in 1910 and 1970 are Metal Dogs, those born in 1922 and 1982 are Water Dogs, and so on.

## Metal Dog: 1910, 1970
The Metal Dog is bold, confident and forthright, and sets about everything he does in a resolute and determined manner. He has a great belief in his abilities and has no hesitation about speaking his mind or devoting himself to some just cause. He can be rather serious at times and can get anxious and irritable when things are not going according to plan. He tends to have very specific interests and it would certainly help him to broaden his outlook and also become more involved in group activities. He is extremely loyal and faithful to his friends.

## Water Dog: 1922, 1982
The Water Dog has a very direct and outgoing personality. He is an excellent communicator and has little trouble in persuading others to fall in with his plans. He does, however, have a somewhat carefree nature and is not as disciplined or as thorough as he should be in certain matters. Neither does he keep as much control over his finances as he should, but he can be most generous to his family and friends and will make sure that they want for nothing. The Water Dog is usually very good with children and has a wide circle of friends.

## Wood Dog: 1934
This Dog is a hard and conscientious worker and will usually make a favourable impression wherever he goes.

He is less independent than some of the other types of Dog and prefers to work in a group rather than on his own. He is popular, has a good sense of humour, and takes a very keen interest in the activities of the various members of his family. He is often attracted to the finer things in life and can get much pleasure from collecting stamps, coins, pictures or antiques. He also prefers to live in the country rather than the town.

**Fire Dog: 1946**
This Dog has a lively outgoing personality and is able to establish friendships with remarkable ease. He is an honest and conscientious worker and likes to take an active part in all that is going on around him. He also likes to explore new ideas and providing he can get the necessary support and advice, he can often succeed where others have failed. He does, however, have a tendency to be stubborn, and providing he can overcome this, the Fire Dog can often achieve considerable fame and fortune.

**Earth Dog: 1898, 1958**
The Earth Dog is very talented and astute. He is methodical and efficient and is capable of going far in his chosen profession. He tends to be rather quiet and reserved but has a very persuasive manner and usually secures his objectives without too much opposition. He is generous and kind and is always ready to lend a helping hand when it is needed. He is also held in very high esteem by his friends and colleagues and he is usually most dignified in his appearance.

# Prospects for the Dog in 1992

The Chinese New Year starts on 4 February 1992. Until then the old year, the year of the Goat, is still making its presence felt.

The year of the Goat (15 February 1991-3 February 1992) could well have been rather frustrating and awkward for the Dog. He is unlikely to have made as much progress as he would have liked, and he could have felt that his efforts and work have passed unnoticed and that he has not received the credit he is due. He could also have experienced some financial problems over the year.

The Dog can take heart, however. His prospects will soon improve and his efforts in the year of the Goat will certainly not have been wasted. Provided that in the closing stages of the year he continues to set about his activities to the best of his abilities and remains patient and diplomatic, he will soon notice an upturn in his fortunes. Those around him will begin to look more favourably on his ideas, he will find it easier to accomplish things, and many Dogs can look forward to receiving some good news to do with their work and future prospects early in 1992. He should remain particularly alert to opportunities in January and February.

His domestic and social life over the year of the Goat is likely to have been most pleasant, and the Dog can look forward to having some good times with his family and friends around Christmas and the New Year. Romance is also very well aspected for single Dogs, and for those Dogs who are unattached or are seeking new friends the closing stages of the year are a most auspicious time. The single Dog would do well to attend as many social occasions as he can, as the prospects for making new friends at this time are most favourable.

The year of the Monkey starts on 4 February 1992 and it is going to be a busy but pleasant year for the Dog. He can look forward to making substantial progress in his work and this is likely to compensate for any difficulties or setbacks he might have experienced in recent years. He should actively pursue any opportunities that arise and should act in a positive, determined and persistent manner. The rewards for the Dog in the year of the

Monkey can be great, with the prospects of a better and more rewarding job and the possible realization of some of his ambitions. However, the amount of success that he enjoys will depend on his efforts and degree of determination.

In addition to doing well in his work, financial matters are also well aspected. Any financial problems that he might have been experiencing will certainly be eased over the year, and the Dog would do well to seriously consider putting any spare funds that he might have in a savings policy, particularly in one that would make provision for his long-term future.

The Dog is, however, likely to incur some expenses over the year in connection with his property, either through carrying out alterations or moving. In either case, the Dog should keep a close watch on all the costs involved and pay particular attention to any documents and forms that he might have to sign. An overlooked detail could result in delays, unnecessary expense and a lot of correspondence.

The Dog's domestic life will be generally happy and settled over the year. There is a slight danger however that because of the many demands on his time or his preoccupation with his work he will not involve his family in his activities as much as he should, and this is a point that all Dogs would do well to watch.

He will also lead a busy social life over the year, and while there are some Dogs who are not keen socializers and prefer to keep themselves to themselves, all Dogs should make an effort to go out more and particularly to accept any invitations to social events that they receive. These are not only likely to prove most enjoyable occasions but could easily lead to new friendships and to the widening of the Dog's circle of acquaintances, all of which will be very much to his advantage.

There will be several opportunities for the Dog to travel over the year—sometimes at short notice—and he is likely to find any travelling he undertakes most pleasurable. He will also enjoy his main holiday of the year.

The Dog will enjoy generally good health over 1992, although he should make sure that he eats a healthy and well balanced diet and, as far as possible, avoids rushing his food. If he does not, he could suffer from digestive problems which, although not serious, could nevertheless cause him some discomfort.

Generally however, 1992 will be a most pleasing year for the Dog. He will do very well in his work and with financial matters, and he will be much in demand with his family and friends. However, because of the many demands on his time, the Dog will need to ensure that he devotes sufficient time and attention to his family, and he should avoid getting too pre-occupied with his own concerns. Provided he bears these things in mind, 1992 will be a happy, successful, and most prosperous year for him.

As far as the different types of Dog are concerned, 1992 will be a busy and eventful year for the **Metal Dog**. Many will have cause for a personal celebration over the year— either through an engagement, wedding or a birth. Indeed, socially and domestically the Metal Dog will lead a very happy life. Even those Metal Dogs who may have been passing through periods of uncertainty or who have felt lonely in recent years will notice a distinct improvement in their fortunes. The Metal Dog will also do well in his work; many will obtain a better and more lucrative position over the year. He should remain alert for any opportunities, and even if, as is likely, he does meet with the occasional setback, he must not be deterred from pursuing his objectives and ambitions. His achievements over the year will be on the whole quite considerable. However there will be many demands made upon his time, and should he feel under pressure he should not hesitate to ask for support and assistance from others. Putting himself under too much strain—and the Metal Dog is not helped in this by his tendency to worry—could undermine his own efforts and success, and with the omens looking so favourable for him in 1992 this would be a great shame. The Metal Dog is also likely to travel considerable distances in 1992.

This will be a good year for the **Water Dog**. He will be able to devote much time over the year to his hobbies and interests, and these are likely to give him a great deal of pleasure. He can also look forward to an active social life in 1992, and any Water Dog who may have felt lonely in recent years should make every effort to go out more, perhaps joining a local society or a club specializing in one of his interests. With a little effort his circle of friends will widen appreciably. The Water Dog will be fortunate in financial matters over the year, and many Water Dogs will receive a sum of money from the fruition of an old investment or from an unexpected source. The Water Dog could also enjoy luck in some competitions that he enters. However, despite the good financial fortune that he will enjoy, he should keep a watchful eye on his outgoings and should be wary about making any large purchase or entering into any transaction against his better judgement. When in doubt it would be worth seeking the advice of others. The Water Dog will travel considerable distances over the year, and many will be able to visit friends and relatives living some distance away, or will visit places that they have wanted to see for a long time. The travelling he undertakes will be most pleasurable, and the whole year will be one that he will be able to look back on with much fondness and satisfaction.

This will be a successful year for the **Wood Dog**, and he is likely to make progress in many of his activities. In his work he should pursue any opportunities that come his way; with a determined and positive outlook he will be surprised and delighted at just how much he can achieve. In addition to doing well in his work he should also give some thought to his future aspirations—the ideas that he comes up with could prove to be of great significance in the future. The Wood Dog will also be generally fortunate in financial matters over the year, although any Wood Dog who may have been experiencing financial problems would be helped by conducting a review of his level of expenditure and, if possible, by trying to put a skill or some knowledge that he has to profitable use. He will be pleased by what just a little effort on his part can achieve. Throughout the year the Wood Dog should set about his activities in a positive and confident attitude. He will lead a pleasant social life over the year, and like the other Dogs he will greatly enjoy the travelling that he undertakes in 1992.

This will be an interesting and successful year for the **Fire Dog**. He will do well in his work, and if he has been thinking of changing his job, seeking promotion or feeling in need of a new challenge, he will find several tempting opportunities on the horizon. In his actions over the year he should be bold and persistent—the rewards of the year of the Monkey can be great for the Fire Dog, but it is up to him to take advantage of the auspicious trends that prevail. He should also advance any ideas that he has—the Fire Dog is quite an imaginative and innovative thinker, and with the year of the Monkey being a year favouring enterprise and initiative, the Fire Dog will be pleased with how his ideas and proposals are received. However, in view of the success and progress he will make in his work, the demands on his time will be quite considerable, and in the interests of domestic harmony the Fire Dog should ensure that he devotes sufficient time to the interests and activities of the various members of his family. Indeed, domestic, family and social matters are all well aspected for the Fire Dog, and providing he gets his priorities right 1992 will be one of the most enjoyable and successful years he has had in a long time.

This will be a pleasing year for the **Earth Dog**, although to take advantage of the favourable trends that exist he will need to have some idea of his objectives for the year and to set himself some goal to aim for. Whether it is a better job, changing his accommodation or achieving some personal ambition, all are possible but the Earth Dog must know what he wants and work purposefully towards his objective. Once he has set himself some goals he will be delighted by the progress that he is able to make and the success that he will enjoy. The Earth Dog will find any financial problems he may have been experiencing will be eased considerably over the course of the year, and he could enjoy some luck in a financial matter towards the end of 1992. The Earth Dog's domestic life will be very busy over the year with many family commitments and a possible increase in his responsibilities, but he can look forward to having some truly splendid and memorable times with his family and friends.

## Action Plan for the Dog in 1992

This will be a much improved year for you and you will enjoy success in many of your activities. However you would do well to sort out your priorities for the year and also to have a set of objectives to aim for. Be positive and determined in your actions and go after the opportunities that you see—with the right attitude your efforts, skills, and talents will be rewarded. Also, remember that in the year of the Monkey good fortune will particularly favour those who are bold and enterprising.

Do involve your family and friends in your activities, for although as with any year there will naturally be setbacks or problems you will have to overcome, try to deal with any troubles that arise calmly and rationally, and if need be seek the advice of others.

While there will be many demands made on your time, do make sure that you do not get so preoccupied with your work and other interests that you neglect personal relationships. Make sure you spend as much time with your loved ones as you can, and make this, the year of the Monkey, one of the best years you have had for a long time.

Travel is particularly well aspected for the year, and if there is some faraway destination you would like to visit, or you have some relatives living some distance away, this could be an ideal year to make such a journey.

# Famous Dogs

Kingsley Amis, Jane Asher, Kenneth Baker, Brigitte Bardot, Dr Christiaan Barnard, Lionel Blair, Simon le Bon, David Bowie, Peter Brooke, Kate Bush, Max Bygraves, King Carl Gustaf XVI of Sweden, Belinda Carlisle, Cher, Leonard Cohen, Sir Winston Churchill, Henry Cooper, Edwina Currie, Jamie Lee Curtis, Timothy Dalton, Charles Dance, Christopher Dean, Claude Debussy, John Dunn, Sally Field, Zsa Zsa Gabor, Judy Garland, Bamber Gascoigne, George Gershwin, Lenny Henry, Frankie Howerd, Victor Hugo, Barry Humphries, Michael Jackson, Henry Kelly, Felicity Kendal, Nik Kershaw, Sue Lawley, Sophia Loren, Joanna Lumley, Shirley MacLaine, Madonna, Norman Mailer, Barry Manilow, Rik Mayall, Simon Mayo, Golda Meir, Freddie Mercury, Liza Minnelli, David Niven, Gary Numan, Michelle Pfeiffer, Sydney Pollack, Elvis Presley, Anneka Rice, Malcolm Rifkind, Paul Robeson, Linda Ronstadt, Gabriella Sabatini, Carl Sagan, Sylvester Stallone, Robert Louis Stevenson, David Suchet, Donald Sutherland, Mother Teresa, Voltaire, Prince William, Ian Woosnam.

# The Pig

| | | | |
|---|---|---|---|
| 30 January 1911 | to | 17 February 1912 | *Metal Pig* |
| 16 February 1923 | to | 4 February 1924 | *Water Pig* |
| 4 February 1935 | to | 23 January 1936 | *Wood Pig* |
| 22 January 1947 | to | 9 February 1948 | *Fire Pig* |
| 8 February 1959 | to | 27 January 1960 | *Earth Pig* |
| 27 January 1971 | to | 14 February 1972 | *Metal Pig* |
| 13 February 1983 | to | 1 February 1984 | *Water Pig* |

## The Personality of the Pig

It is not enough merely to exist. It's not enough to say, 'I'm earning enough to live and to support my family. I do my work well. I'm a good father. I'm a good husband. I'm a good churchgoer.' That's all very well. But you must do something more. Seek always to do some good, somewhere. Every man has to seek in his own way to make his own self more noble and to realize his own true worth. You must give some time to your fellow man.

*—Albert Schweitzer: a Pig*

The Pig is born under the sign of honesty. He has a kind and understanding nature and is well-known for his abilities as a peace-maker. He hates any sort of discord or unpleasantness and will do all in his power to sort out differences of opinion or bring opposing factions together.

He is an excellent conversationalist and speaks truthfully and to the point. He dislikes any form of falsehood or hypocrisy and is a firm believer in justice and the maintenance of law and order. In spite of these beliefs, however, the Pig is reasonably tolerant and often prepared to forgive others for their wrongs. The Pig rarely harbours grudges and is never vindictive.

The Pig is usually very popular. He enjoys other people's company and likes to be involved in joint or group activities. He will be a loyal member of any club or society and can be relied upon to lend a helping hand at functions. He is also an excellent fund-raiser for charities and is often a great supporter of humanitarian causes.

The Pig is a hard and conscientious worker and is particularly respected for his reliability and integrity. In his early years he will try his hand at several different jobs, but he is usually happiest where he feels that he is being of service to others. He will unselfishly give up his time for the common good and is highly valued by his colleagues and employers.

The Pig has a good sense of humour and invariably has a smile, joke, or some whimsical remark at the ready. He loves to entertain and to please others, and there are many who have been attracted to careers in showbusiness or who enjoy following the careers of famous stars and personalities.

There are, unfortunately, some who take advantage of the Pig's good nature and impose on his generosity. The Pig has great difficulty in saying 'no' and, although he may dislike being firm, it would be in his own interest to say occasionally, 'enough is enough'. The Pig can also be rather naïve and gullible; if at any stage in his life he feels that he has been badly let down, he will make sure that it will never happen again and will try to become self-reliant. There are many Pigs who have become entrepreneurs or forged a successful career on their own after some early disappointment in life. And although the Pig tends to spend his money quite freely, he is usually very astute in financial matters and there are many Pigs who have become wealthy.

Another characteristic of the Pig is his ability to recover from setbacks reasonably quickly. His faith and his strength of character keep him going. If he thinks that there is a job he can do—or has something that he wants to achieve—he will pursue it with a dogged determination. He can also be stubborn and, no matter how many may plead with him, once he has made his mind up he will rarely change his views.

Although the Pig may work hard he also knows how to enjoy himself. He is a great pleasure-seeker and will quite happily spend his hard-earned money on a lavish holiday, an expensive meal (for the Pig is a connoisseur of good food and wine) or take part in a variety of recreational activities. He also enjoys small social gatherings and, if he is in company which he likes, the Pig can very easily become the life and soul of the party. He does, however, tend to become rather withdrawn at larger functions or when among strangers.

The Pig is also a creature of comfort and his home will usually be fitted with all the latest in luxury appliances. Where possible, he will prefer to live in the country to the town and will opt to have a big garden—for the Pig is usually a keen and successful gardener.

The Pig is very popular with the opposite sex and will often have numerous romances before he settles down. Once settled, however, he will be loyal and protective to his partner and he will find that he is especially well-suited to those born under the signs of the Goat, Rabbit, Dog, Tiger, and another Pig. Due to his affable and easy-going nature he can also establish a satisfactory relationship with the remaining signs of the Chinese zodiac, with the exception of the Snake. The Snake tends to be wily, secretive, and very guarded, and this can be intensely irritating to the honest and open-hearted Pig.

The lady Pig will devote all her energies to the needs of her children and her partner. She tries to ensure that they want for nothing, and their pleasure is very much her pleasure. Her home will either be very clean and orderly or hopelessly untidy. Strangely, there seems to be no middle ground with the Pig—they either love housework or detest it! She does, however, have considerable talents as an organizer, and this, combined with her friendly and open manner, enables her to secure many of her objectives. She can also be a caring and conscientious parent and has very good taste in clothes.

The Pig is usually lucky in life and will rarely want for anything. Provided he does not let others take advantage of his good nature and is not afraid of asserting himself, the Pig will go through life making friends, helping others, and winning the admiration of many.

# The Five Different Types of Pig

In addition to the twelve signs of the Chinese zodiac, there are five elements, and these have a strengthening or moderating influence on the sign. The effects of the five elements on the Pig are described below, together with the years that the elements were exercising their influence. Therefore all Pigs born in 1911 and 1971 are Metal Pigs, those born in 1923 and 1983 are Water Pigs, and so on.

## Metal Pig: 1911, 1971
The Metal Pig is more ambitious and determined than some of the other types of Pig. He is strong, energetic, and likes to be involved in a wide variety of different activities. He is very open and forthright in his views, although he can be a little too trusting at times and has a tendency to accept things at face value. He has a good sense of humour and loves to attend parties and other social gatherings. He has a warm, outgoing nature and usually has a large circle of friends.

## Water Pig: 1923, 1983

The Water Pig has a heart of gold. He is generous and loyal and tries to remain on good terms with everyone. He will do his utmost to help others, but sadly there are some who will take advantage of his kind nature and he should, in his own interests, be a little more discriminating and be prepared to stand firm against anything that he does not like. Although he prefers the quieter things in life, he has a wide range of interests. He particularly enjoys outdoor pursuits and attending parties and social occasions. He is a hard and conscientious worker and invariably does well in his chosen profession. He is also gifted in the art of communication.

## Wood Pig: 1935

This Pig has a friendly, persuasive manner and is easily able to gain the confidence of others. He likes to be involved in all that is going on around him and can sometimes take on more responsibility than he can properly handle at any one time. He is loyal to his family and friends and he also derives much pleasure from helping those less fortunate than himself. The Wood Pig is usually an optimist and leads a very full, enjoyable, and satisfying life. He also has a good sense of humour.

## Fire Pig: 1947

The Fire Pig is both energetic and adventurous and he sets about everything he does in a confident and resolute manner. He is very forthright in his views and does not mind taking risks in order to achieve his objectives. He can, however, get carried away by the excitement of the moment and ought to exercise more caution with some of the enterprises with which he gets involved. The Fire Pig is usually lucky in money matters and is well-known for his generosity. He is also very caring towards the members of his family.

**Earth Pig: 1899, 1959**

This Pig has a kindly nature. He is sensible and realistic and will go to great lengths in order to please his employers and to secure his aims and ambitions. He is an excellent organizer and is particularly astute in business and financial matters. He has a good sense of humour and a wide circle of friends. He also likes to lead an active social life, although he does sometimes have a tendency to eat and drink more than is good for him.

# Prospects for the Pig in 1992

The Chinese New Year starts on 4 February 1992. Until then the old year, the year of the Goat, is still making its presence felt.

The year of the Goat (15 February 1991–3 February 1992) will have been a pleasant year for the Pig. He is likely to have made progress in his work and, most significantly, he will have gained a lot in experience and this will help his prospects considerably over the next few years.

He is also likely to have been contented and settled in his home life and to have found those around him supportive of his various activities. His social life will also have been most pleasant with romance especially well aspected for the single Pig. Over the year there will have been many opportunities to meet others and build up new friendships, and indeed the latter part of the Goat year will be a busy and happy time socially for the Pig.

Although the last few months of the year could prove expensive, the Pig is likely to purchase several excellent bargains in the January sales, especially items for himself and his home. Also, if he has been considering decorating or carrying out alterations to his home, January and February 1992 would be a good time to start.

The year of the Monkey begins on 4 February 1992 and it is going to be a reasonable year for the Pig. Admittedly not all the events of the year will work out in his favour, and he may have some small and niggling problems to overcome, but to compensate for this the year will still contain some happy and memorable times for him.

Socially this will be an excellent year for the Pig. There will be several very enjoyable functions for him to attend and he will also continue to build up new friendships over the year. All Pigs will find that their circle of friends and acquaintances will increase substantially in 1992. Romance is again very well aspected, and there will be numerous opportunities for the single Pig to meet with others and to make new friends. Any Pigs who may have been lonely in recent years would do well to go out more and meet those who share their interests. With the favourable social trends that prevail, they will be very glad they did so!

The Pig's family will also be most supportive over the year, and the Pig should involve those around him in his various activities. Indeed he can look forward to spending some very happy times with his family in 1992, although he could also, on the other hand, experience a few domestic problems in the year. These could involve a clash of interests, or maybe arise from the Pig's concern about the activities and well-being of someone close to him. If such a situation occurs, the Pig should be his usual under-standing and considerate self, but at the same time he should not hesitate to express his views and feelings on any matter that might be causing him concern. With good will and common sense on both sides, any problems or differences can be sorted out quickly and amicably. This care in handling domestic matters is something that all Pigs will need to bear in mind throughout 1992. If he does not, he could find that the resulting slight discord could take the edge off what will otherwise be a generally pleasant year for him.

The Pig will need to be careful with financial matters in 1992, and it would certainly be in his interests to keep a watchful eye over his level of expenditure. He should also avoid taking any unnecessary risks with his money or entering into any highly speculative venture—1992 is just not a year in which the Pig can afford to take risks. If he does, he could easily end up the loser.

The Pig will make a reasonable amount of progress in his work and there will be some interesting opportunities and openings for him to pursue. However, in all his actions the Pig should make sure that he has the support of others and avoids acting independently. Similarly, if he has any idea or scheme that he wishes to advance, he needs to make sure that he first has the backing of others. 1992 is a year when the Pig needs to act in conjunction with others rather than on his own, and if he bears this in mind he will find his progress greater and more satisfactory than if he maintained an independent stance.

Any Pig who is in an occupation that involves the use of his creative talents is likely to do well, and he should use any opportunity to promote himself and his work. The year of the Monkey is very much a year that favours creativity and enterprise, and any Pig who is a particularly innovative thinker or who has some artistic leaning could do extremely well. In addition to success in creative matters, the Pig could also find outdoor activities especially satisfying, and for those Pigs who like gardening, walking or who are sporting enthusiasts, the year could hold many happy moments.

Generally 1992 will be quite a pleasant year for the Pig. Provided he exercises a certain amount of caution in financial matters and handles any domestic problems that may arise with care, he will enjoy the year of the Monkey. He will make reasonable progress in most of his activities, and the happy times that he can look forward to with his family and friends will make up for any small problems that he might have had to overcome during the year.

As far as the different types of Pig are concerned, 1992 will be an interesting and varied year for the **Metal Pig**. He will make reasonably good progress in his work, and those Metal Pigs seeking employment should pursue any opportunities that they see—their determination will be rewarded, and any qualifications and additional skills the Metal Pig can obtain over the year will prove very useful in the future. Socially and romantically 1992 will be a highly favourable year for him, although he still needs to handle his relationships with care. He should take the views and feelings of those around him into account, and if he meets with any opposition to his plans, he should show himself to be conciliatory and flexible. He would do well to bear in mind any advice he is given over the year, particularly that from his family and colleagues. He needs to be careful in financial matters and should make sure that he understands the terms of any financial transaction that he might be considering. If he plans any large purchase over the year he would do well to look around and compare as many prices as he can. By doing so he will be able to make significant savings. The Metal Pig will enjoy any travelling that he undertakes over the year.

1992 will generally be a good year for the **Water Pig**, although he may have one or two minor problems to contend with. These problems are unlikely to be serious, but it would be very much in his interests to discuss any worries or problems that he might have with those around him. Sometimes the Water Pig can be guilty of keeping his feelings to himself—particularly as he does not like to trouble others—but throughout the year he would be helped if he were more open and prepared to discuss any problems or worries that he might have. He will feel considerably better for doing so and throughout 1992 he will find much truth in the saying, 'a problem shared is a problem halved.' The Water Pig should also stand firm against doing anything that runs contrary to his better judgement or to being pressurized into making a hasty decision. He can occasionally give in to others far too easily, and this could lead to unhappiness. In 1992 he should be prepared to stand his ground. However, despite any problems that may occur over the year the Water Pig will lead a most pleasant social life, and any Water Pig who may have felt lonely in recent years should make every effort to go out more and if possible join a local club or society. He will also derive much pleasure from outdoor activities over the year, and if he has any creative skills, or wishes to develop such skills, he is likely to obtain immense satisfaction from this. Indeed his skills and talents will be viewed favourably by others and could even result in an additional source of income.

This will be a challenging year for the **Wood Pig** and he will need to exercise care and caution with many of his activities. Through no fault of his own the Wood Pig could find some of his plans disrupted or needing to be rearranged; he could also meet with opposition from some colleagues or business associates. However any problems that he may have to face will be over in the first few months of the year, and the one thing that the Wood Pig should not do is get too disheartened by any awkward problems that he will have to overcome. None of these problems are likely to be serious and most can easily be got round with tact and good common sense. Indeed he should view any problems as challenges to be surmounted and triumphed over. He should also remember that he has many good friends to whom he can turn for help and advice; he will certainly be encouraged by the support and assistance that others are prepared to give him. The Wood Pig will lead a very full social life over the year and will attend some most enjoyable parties and functions. He could also be involved in arranging a reunion with family or friends, and this again is likely to give him much pleasure. The Wood Pig would also do well to give some thought to his long-term future—the ideas he comes up with will prove most significant over the next few years.

The **Fire Pig** will enjoy 1992, and while not all the events of the year will work out entirely in his favour, the year will still hold some worthwhile opportunities for him to pursue. He should not hesitate to promote any ideas that he has, and with his outgoing and personable nature he is likely to impress many around him and win the support of others. However, before embarking on any new venture it would be in his interests to make sure that he has the backing of others. To act independently or without support could easily leave him isolated and in a difficult position. The Fire Pig should also avoid being committed to too many undertakings at any one time or getting involved in any arguments or contentious discussions—an ill-timed remark could easily rebound on him and inflame his relationships with others needlessly. When faced with any problems over the year he should tackle them determinedly, decisively and diplomatically. Like many Pigs in 1992 the Fire Pig could also experience a few problems and worries in domestic matters; as far as possible he should deal with these as soon as they arise and with his usual good common sense. However, despite any problems that occur, the Fire Pig can still look forward to having some splendid times with his family and friends and also to being involved in a major family celebration over the year.

This will be a busy year for the **Earth Pig**, and he is likely to find that family and domestic matters will take up much of his spare time. Although this could involve sorting out some rather awkward domestic problems, the problems themselves are likely to be short-lived and generally throughout the year he can look forward to leading a happy home life. He will also be particularly delighted over the year by the achievements and accomplishments of a younger relation. The Earth Pig does, however, need to deal with financial matters with extreme care in 1992, keeping a watchful eye on his level of expenditure. He should also be wary about committing himself to any large financial venture without checking the clauses and, if applicable, the terms of repayment very carefully. An oversight could prove costly for him. The Earth Pig will make a reasonable amount of progress in his work and he should look out for new opportunities to pursue, especially in the latter months of the year. Any Earth Pig with creative talents and skills should promote his work as much as he can as it is likely to be most favourably received. Although the Earth Pig will be kept quite busy over the year, he should remember that he has many good friends to turn to for support and advice; he will find that they will be only too pleased to help him in any way they can. The Earth Pig would also do well to make sure that he gets away for at least one good holiday over the year, and if possible, to take several short breaks at different times of the year. He will find these will do him a considerable amount of good.

## Action Plan for the Pig in 1992

To achieve the best results this year you need to take great care with your relationships with others. Avoid unpleasant scenes (which as a Pig you dislike anyway) and bear in mind the views and feelings of those around you. Try to involve others—especially your family—in your activities, and avoid acting independently.

Continue to work to the best of your abilities. If you have any creative leanings, make every effort to promote yourself and your skills in any way you can. Your efforts will be rewarded.

Be prudent in financial matters.

Tackle any problems that arise with your usual good sense, and do not forget that you have many good friends to whom you can turn for advice.

Although this may not be the best of years for you, it certainly need not be a bad one. Your social life is very well aspected and your circle of friends is likely to increase substantially. If you set about your activities carefully and sensibly you will not go far wrong, and the experience and skills that you gain and the contacts you build up will be very much to your future advantage.

# Famous Pigs

Russ Abbot, Woody Allen, Julie Andrews, Fred Astaire, Sir Richard Attenborough, Gerhard Berger, Humphrey Bogart, Maria Callas, Dr George Carey, Richard Chamberlain, Brian Clough, Noël Coward, Oliver Cromwell, the Dalai Lama, Sir Robin Day, Lord Denning, Sheena Easton, Ralph Waldo Emerson, David Essex, Farrah Fawcett, Debbie Greenwood, Emmylou Harris, William Randolph Hearst, Ernest Hemingway, Henry VIII, Alfred Hitchcock, King Hussein of Jordan, Elton John, C.G. Jung, Stephen King, Henry Kissinger, Jerry Lee Lewis, John McEnroe, Marcel Marceau, Ngaio Marsh, Johnny Mathis, Robert Maxwell, Montgomery of Alamein, Dudley Moore, Patrick Moore, John Mortimer, Mozart, Michael Parkinson, Luciano Pavarotti, Lester Piggot, Dan Quayle, Maurice Ravel, Ronald Reagan, John D. Rockefeller, Ginger Rogers, Nick Ross, Salman Rushdie, Baroness Sue Ryder of Warsaw, Sade, Arantxa Sanchez, Telly Savalas, Albert Schweitzer, Donald Sinden, Steven Spielberg, Tracey Ullman, the Duchess of York.

# Appendix

The relationship between the twelve animal signs—both on a personal level and business level—is an important aspect of Chinese horoscopes and in this appendix the compatibility between the signs is shown in the two tables that follow. Also included in this appendix are the names of the signs ruling the hours of the day and from this it is possible to find your ascendant and discover yet another aspect of your personality.

# Personal Relationships

*Key*

1 Excellent. Great rapport.
2 A successful relationship. Many interests in common.
3 Mutual respect and understanding. A good relationship.
4 Fair. Needs care and some willingness to compromise in order for the relationship to work.
5 Awkward. Possible difficulties in communication with few interests in common.
6 A clash of personalities. Very difficult.

| | Rat | Ox | Tiger | Rabbit | Dragon | Snake | Horse | Goat | Monkey | Rooster | Dog | Pig |
|---|---|---|---|---|---|---|---|---|---|---|---|---|
| Rat | 1 | | | | | | | | | | | |
| Ox | 1 | 3 | | | | | | | | | | |
| Tiger | 4 | 6 | 5 | | | | | | | | | |
| Rabbit | 5 | 2 | 3 | 3 | | | | | | | | |
| Dragon | 1 | 5 | 5 | 3 | 2 | | | | | | | |
| Snake | 3 | 1 | 6 | 2 | 1 | 5 | | | | | | |
| Horse | 6 | 5 | 1 | 4 | 3 | 4 | 2 | | | | | |
| Goat | 5 | 5 | 3 | 1 | 4 | 3 | 2 | 2 | | | | |
| Monkey | 1 | 3 | 6 | 3 | 1 | 3 | 5 | 3 | 1 | | | |
| Rooster | 4 | 1 | 4 | 6 | 2 | 1 | 2 | 4 | 5 | 5 | | |
| Dog | 3 | 4 | 1 | 3 | 6 | 3 | 2 | 5 | 3 | 5 | 2 | |
| Pig | 2 | 3 | 2 | 2 | 3 | 6 | 3 | 2 | 2 | 3 | 1 | 2 |

# Business Relationships

*Key*
1  Excellent. Marvellous understanding and rapport.
2  Very good. Complement each other well.
3  A good working relationship and understanding can be developed.
4  Fair, but compromise and a common objective is often needed for this relationship to work.
5  Awkward. Unlikely to work, either through lack of trust, understanding or the competitiveness of the signs.
6  Mistrust. Difficult. To be avoided.

| | Rat | Ox | Tiger | Rabbit | Dragon | Snake | Horse | Goat | Monkey | Rooster | Dog | Pig |
|---|---|---|---|---|---|---|---|---|---|---|---|---|
| Rat | 2 | | | | | | | | | | | |
| Ox | 1 | 3 | | | | | | | | | | |
| Tiger | 3 | 6 | 5 | | | | | | | | | |
| Rabbit | 4 | 3 | 4 | 3 | | | | | | | | |
| Dragon | 1 | 4 | 3 | 4 | 3 | | | | | | | |
| Snake | 3 | 2 | 6 | 4 | 1 | 5 | | | | | | |
| Horse | 6 | 4 | 1 | 4 | 3 | 4 | 3 | | | | | |
| Goat | 4 | 5 | 3 | 1 | 4 | 3 | 3 | 2 | | | | |
| Monkey | 2 | 3 | 4 | 5 | 1 | 5 | 4 | 4 | 3 | | | |
| Rooster | 5 | 1 | 5 | 5 | 2 | 1 | 2 | 5 | 4 | 6 | | |
| Dog | 4 | 5 | 2 | 3 | 6 | 3 | 2 | 5 | 3 | 5 | 3 | |
| Pig | 3 | 3 | 2 | 2 | 4 | 5 | 4 | 2 | 3 | 4 | 3 | 3 |

# Your Ascendant

The ascendant has a very strong influence on your personality and together with the information already given about your sign and the effects of the element on your sign, it will help you to build up an even greater insight of your true personality according to Chinese horoscopes.

The hours of the day are named after the twelve animal signs and the sign governing the time you were born is your ascendant. To find your ascendant, look up the time of your birth on the table below, bearing in mind any local time differences in the place you were born.

| | |
|---|---|
| 11 p.m. to  1 a.m. | The hours of the Rat |
| 1 a.m. to  3 a.m. | The hours of the Ox |
| 3 a.m. to  5 a.m. | The hours of the Tiger |
| 5 a.m. to  7 a.m. | The hours of the Rabbit |
| 7 a.m. to  9 a.m. | The hours of the Dragon |
| 9 a.m. to 11 a.m. | The hours of the Snake |
| 11 a.m. to  1 p.m. | The hours of the Horse |
| 1 p.m. to  3 p.m. | The hours of the Goat |
| 3 p.m. to  5 p.m. | The hours of the Monkey |
| 5 p.m. to  7 p.m. | The hours of the Rooster |
| 7 p.m. to  9 p.m. | The hours of the Dog |
| 9 p.m. to 11 p.m. | The hours of the Pig |

**Rat:** The influence of the Rat as ascendant is likely to make the sign more outgoing, sociable, and also more careful with money. A particularly beneficial influence for those born under the sign of the Rabbit, Horse, Monkey and Pig.

**Ox:** The Ox as ascendant has a restraining, cautionary and steadying influence which many signs will benefit from. The ascendant also promotes self-confidence and will power and is an especially good ascendant for those born under the sign of the Tiger, Rabbit, and Goat.

**Tiger:**     This ascendant is a dynamic and stirring influence which makes the sign more outgoing, more action-orientated and more impulsive. A generally favourable ascendant for the Ox, Tiger, Snake and Horse.

**Rabbit:**     The Rabbit as ascendant has a moderating influence making the sign more reflective, serene and discreet. A particularly beneficial influence for the Rat, Dragon, Monkey and Rooster.

**Dragon:**     The Dragon as ascendant gives strength, determination and an added ambition to the sign. A favourable influence for those born under the sign of the Rabbit, Goat, Monkey and Dog.

**Snake:**     The Snake as ascendant can make the sign more reflective, more intuitive and more self-reliant on his abilities. A good influence for the Tiger, Goat and Pig.

**Horse:**     The influence of the Horse will make the sign more adventurous, more daring and, on some occasions, more fickle. Generally a beneficial influence for the Rabbit, Snake, Dog and Pig.

**Goat:**     This ascendant will make the sign more tolerant, easy-going and receptive. The Goat could also impart some creative and artistic qualities on the sign. An especially good influence for the Ox, Dragon, Snake and Rooster.

**Monkey:** The Monkey as ascendant is likely to impart a delicious sense of humour and fun to the sign. He will make the sign more enterprising and outgoing—a particularly good influence for the Rat, Ox, Snake and Goat.

**Rooster:** The Rooster as ascendant helps to give the sign a lively, outgoing and very methodical manner. Its influence will increase efficiency and is a good influence for the Ox, Tiger, Rabbit and Horse.

**Dog:** The Dog as ascendant makes the sign more reasonable and fair-minded as well as giving an added a sense of loyalty. A very good ascendant for the Tiger, Dragon, and Goat.

**Pig:** The influence of the Pig can make the sign more sociable, content and self-indulgent. It is also a caring influence and one which can make the sign want to help others. A good ascendant for the Dragon and Monkey.